M000211151

SUCCESSONOMICS

VOLUME 3

Copyright © 2021 CelebrityPress® LLC

All rights reserved. No part of this book may be used or reproduced in any manner whatsoever without prior written consent of the author, except as provided by the United States of America copyright law.

Published by CelebrityPress®, Orlando, FL.

CelebrityPress® is a registered trademark.

Printed in the United States of America.

ISBN: 978-1-7369881-1-4
LCCN: 2021909955

This publication is designed to provide accurate and authoritative information with regard to the subject matter covered. It is sold with the understanding that the publisher is not engaged in rendering legal, accounting, or other professional advice. If legal advice or other expert assistance is required, the services of a competent professional should be sought. The opinions expressed by the authors in this book are not endorsed by CelebrityPress® and are the sole responsibility of the author rendering the opinion.

Most CelebrityPress® titles are available at special quantity discounts for bulk purchases for sales promotions, premiums, fundraising, and educational use. Special versions or book excerpts can also be created to fit specific needs.

For more information, please write:

CelebrityPress®
520 N. Orlando Ave, #2
Winter Park, FL 32789
or call 1.877.261.4930

Visit us online at: www.CelebrityPressPublishing.com

SUCCESS**O**NOMICS

VOLUME 3

LIBRARY OF
CONGRESS
SURPLUS
DUPLICATE

CelebrityPress®
Winter Park, Florida

CONTENTS

CHAPTER 1

SUCCESS-ONOMICS: USE THE POWER OF FOCUS TO ACHIEVE EXCEPTIONAL RESULTS

By Jack Canfield 11

CHAPTER 2

THE STRATEGY OF SUCCESS

By Richard Tyler 23

CHAPTER 3

AN ACCIDENTAL GIFT

By Nora Chahbazi 33

CHAPTER 4

BUILDING RELATIONSHIPS AND RESULTS

By Sabrina Walker Hernandez 43

CHAPTER 5

GOING AFTER WHAT YOU WANT

CHANGING YOUR MINDSET AND SHOWING UP FOR
YOURSELF

By Daniel Mangena 53

CHAPTER 6

YOUR THREE KEYS TO SUCCESS

YOUR STORY - YOUR MINDSET - YOUR WHY

By Ellie D. Shefi 63

CHAPTER 7

THE WITNESS

By Geetha Krishnamurthi 73

CHAPTER 8

**YOUR DIGITAL DNA: THE BUILDING
BLOCKS OF YOUR ONLINE SUCCESS**

By Nick Nanton & JW Dicks 83

CHAPTER 9

MENTAL-SWITCH

HOW I OVERCAME MY DEPRESSION AND CREATED
MASSIVE SUCCESS IN BUSINESS AND LIFE

By Nidhika Bahl 95

CHAPTER 10

I GET KNOCKED DOWN, *BUT* I GET UP AGAIN

By Ilya Vita 107

CHAPTER 11

THE ACCIDENTAL GIFT

By Teresa Morris, DDS 115

CHAPTER 12

BE YOUR BETTER SELF

By Emigdio M. Arias 123

CHAPTER 13

EMPOWERING YOUR WAY TO EMOTIONAL FREEDOM

By Kim Silverman 133

CHAPTER 14

HOPE IS A NARROW BLADE OF GRASS

By Kandiee Campbell 143

CHAPTER 15

THE ABUNDANT LIFE

By Rosie Gregerson Schueller 151

CHAPTER 1

SUCCESS-ONOMICS: USE THE POWER OF FOCUS TO ACHIEVE EXCEPTIONAL RESULTS

BY JACK CANFIELD

Stay focused, believe that you can achieve
at the highest level, surround yourself with others
who believe in you, and do not stray from your goal.
~ Zach Ertz
[Celebrated American football player for the Super Bowl-winning
Philadelphia Eagles]

Focus. It's what helps successful people achieve exceptional results in their lives. And, in choosing this focused path, they follow a set of timeless principles that have been used throughout history by other successful people. When applied, followed and incorporated into your daily life, these principles can bring about the success you are seeking—and very often deliver better results than you ever imagined.

For more than 40 years, I've studied and used these principles to achieve incredible results in my own life. More than 15 years ago,

I wrote a book called *The Success Principles* to catalog them for aspiring achievers everywhere.

So what are just a few of these core habits, attitudes, and strategies that the world's top entrepreneurs use to get results in their careers, finances, lifestyle and more?

THE POWER OF FOCUS

Successful people don't always start with lots of money or high-level connections or other privileged circumstances, but they do stay focused on results that matter. They know which achievements will upgrade their life, and they stay focused on accomplishing those goals. They research the steps, make plans, take action, and persevere until the results they want are achieved.

But they also recognize what they're good at. They stay in their lane. And they delegate everything else.

Focus on Your Unique Skills and Talents

I believe you have inside of you some unique ability or area of brilliance—some one thing you love to do and do so well, you hardly feel like charging people for it. It's effortless for you and a whole lot of fun. And if you could make money doing it, you'd make it your life's work.

Successful people believe this, too. That's why they put their core genius first. They focus on it. And they delegate everything else.

Compare that to the rest of the world who go through life doing everything, even those tasks they're bad at or that could be done cheaper, better and faster by someone else. They can't find the time to focus on their area of brilliance because they fail to delegate even the most menial of tasks.

But when you delegate the things you hate doing or those tasks that are so painful that you end up procrastinating, you get to concentrate on what you love to do. You free up your time... you're more productive. And you get to enjoy life more.

The Total Focus Process

To help you clarify what you should spend your time on versus what you should be delegating to others, I recommend an exercise called The Total Focus Process. The intent is to find those few activities which are the best use of your core genius, bring you the most money, and produce the greatest level of enjoyment to your life.

1. *Start by listing those activities that occupy your time,* whether they're business-related, personal or volunteer work. List even small tasks like returning phone calls, running errands or shopping for groceries.
2. *Choose from this list one to three things* you're particularly brilliant at, your special talents, those unique things most other people simply can't do as well as you. Also choose from this list the three activities that generate the most income for you or your company. Any activities that you're brilliant at and that generate the most income are activities you'll want to focus on.
3. *Finally, create a plan for delegating the remaining activities to others.* Delegating takes time to find reliable people and training to make sure they know your needs, but over time you can assign the nonessential tasks on your list until you are doing less of the ones with little payoff—and more of what you're really good at. That's how you create a brilliant career.

Build a Team That Lets You Focus on Your Core Genius

Every high achiever has a powerful team of key staff members, consultants, vendors, and helpers who do the bulk of the work while he or she is free to create new sources of income and new opportunities for success. The world's greatest philanthropists, athletes, entertainers, professionals, and others also have people who manage projects and handle everyday tasks—enabling them to do more for others, hone their craft, practice their sport, and so on.

If you're a business owner or career professional, start training key people to take over the lesser tasks you identified above. If you're a one-person business, start looking for a dynamic number-two person who could handle your projects, book your sales transactions, and completely take over other tasks while you concentrate on what you do best. If philanthropic pursuits or community projects are your "business," there are volunteers you can recruit to help you—including college interns, who may work solely for class credit.

And if you're a stay-at-home parent, your most valuable "staff" will be your house cleaner, your babysitter and other people who can help you get away for time by yourself or with your spouse. A part-time helper can do grocery shopping, get your car washed, pick up the kids or pick up the dry cleaning—all for a modest wage. If you're a single parent, these folks are even more important to your future success.

In addition to business and personal helpers, high achievers typically have a powerful team of *professional* advisors to turn to for support. Today's world is a complicated place. Professional advisors—such as your banker, your lawyers, a high-net-worth certified public accountant, your investment counselor, your doctor, nutritionist, personal trainer, and the leader of your religious organization—can walk you through challenges and opportunities, saving you time, effort and usually money. If you run a business, these advisors are essential.

Build a Network Based on Genuine Relationships

In addition to having a highly trained team, one of the most important skills for success in today's world, especially for entrepreneurs and business owners, is networking. Jim Bunch, the creator of the Ultimate Game of Life, once stated, "Your network will determine your net worth." In my life this has proven to be true. The more time I've spent consciously building and nurturing my network of advisers, colleagues, clients, students and readers, the more successful I have become.

Businesses and careers are built on relationships, and relationships form when people meet and interact with each other over time in an authentic and caring way. As I'm sure you're aware, statistics confirm over and over that people prefer to do business with people they know, like, respect and trust. Nurturing a powerful network will yield results long into the future.

SET GOALS THAT HELP YOU STAY FOCUSED

Extensive study has shown that—once we decide what we want—the brain actually helps us bring about these life-changing results. For instance, experts know that when you give it a goal, the brain triggers its *reticular activating system*—a web of neuro-pathways that filters through the millions of random images, facts and information we're bombarded with each day, then sends to our conscious mind those bits of data that will help us achieve our goals.

When you give the brain an image of something you want to achieve, it will labor around the clock to find ways to achieve the picture you put there. Without a doubt, the brain is a goal-seeking instrument.

Focus on doing the right things instead of a bunch of things.
~ Mike Krieger – Co-founder of Instagram

How Much By When?

Considering that your brain is working for you, it makes sense to be specific about the goals you will focus on. When I teach about goal-setting, I stress the importance of setting goals that are both *measurable and time-specific—how much and by when*.

Measurable—The most powerful goals are those that are *measurable*, both by you and by others. For instance, your goal might be to generate a specific number of new clients for your new consulting firm so you can meet your income goals. By knowing the required number, you can focus on marketing campaigns, referral agreements and other systems that will hit that number.

Time-specific—Your goal should also be *time-specific*. In other words, not only should you state how much you'll earn, but also *by when* you'll earn it. Only with both these units of measure can you determine whether you've achieved your goal. You also become accountable for meeting your deadline.

Finally, by being so specific, you can then focus your attention on the emotions you'll experience when you achieve your goal. Behind every goal is a deeper *why* you want to achieve it. When you focus on that and the emotions you would feel when you achieve it, it strengthens your motivation and your creativity.

When you decide on the model of car you'll buy with your new-found income, the kind of house you'll live in, or which private schools your children will attend, you can't help but feel the positive emotions attached to those images. When you add emotion, color, detail, and features to visualizing your goals, your brain will begin in earnest to seek out ways to fulfill them.

A Breakthrough Goal Can Expand Your Entire Life

Perhaps the true benefit of any goal is that—by pursuing it—you become a more confident, capable person. No one can ever take away the person you become as a result of pursuing your loftiest goals.

In addition to your many weekly and monthly goals, I recommend that you create *one single goal* such that, in the process of achieving it, you expand every aspect of your life—from your finances to your friends, your business success, your lifestyle and more. Wouldn't that be a goal you would want to work on constantly and pursue with enthusiasm?

I call that a Breakthrough Goal.

For instance, if you're a consultant and know that you could land big tech companies as clients by speaking at the annual industry conference, wouldn't you work night and day to achieve that goal?

And if you partnered with smaller consulting firms to provide specific services that you can't do yourself, wouldn't that grow your business, your income, and your status in the industry—leading to other opportunities and a far more important network of connections than you have right now?

It would expand everything you do in your career and amplify who you are as a person. That's an example of a Breakthrough Goal.

FOCUS ON POSSIBILITIES AND BELIEVE IN YOURSELF

What's the ultimate focal point that successful people use to achieve exceptional results? *They believe in themselves.*

They believe that the goals they've set are the right path for them. And they believe that, with enough effort, they'll achieve them. Not only does this belief allow them to focus like never before on creating spectacular outcomes, it often helps them achieve *beyond their original goals.*

How about you?

Do you believe you can accomplish incredible goals and experience outstanding success? Believing in yourself is a choice. It's not always an easy one—in fact, other people will often make you doubt your belief—but it's a choice that you alone must make.

Once you believe in yourself, no goal will be too lofty. No ambition will be out of reach. With enough determination and focus, you'll begin to see the steps necessary to achieve your ideal outcome. You'll even see the Universe conspire in your favor with unexpected opportunities that show up to get you closer to your goal.

So what are some ways to boost your belief in yourself and your future? Positive self-talk, visualization, training, coaching, and the confidence that comes from taking action will increase your belief in your own skills and abilities. And with practice, you can gain the new skills you need, which only further increases your belief in yourself.

Finally, you can borrow the belief others have in you, especially in the beginning while you're still uncertain about taking on that life-changing goal.

Surround Yourself With Positive People

Positive people who are nurturing, empowering, encouraging, and pro-actively helpful will help you see additional possibilities and further believe in yourself. Look for supporters who believe that what you want is possible, but also who applaud you, who are possibility thinkers—and who believe you deserve to succeed at the highest level.

You want people in your life who will say, "Great idea! You can do that! Here's what you'll need. How can I help?"

Positive people coach us. They mentor us. They come through with ideas that help us expand on our goal. They make us believe we can achieve all that and more. And the good news is, positive people are easy to find. Perhaps they're part of your circle right now and might be delighted to spend more time with you. Look around and have the courage to ask them.

* * * *

Only when you focus on your goals and believe they are possible will you begin to see your successes add up to the life of your dreams. There are no limiting factors if you believe in yourself and are willing to take action on your goals.

About Jack

Known as America's #1 Success Coach, Jack Canfield is the CEO of the Canfield Training Group in Santa Barbara, CA, which trains and coaches entrepreneurs, corporate leaders, managers, sales professionals and the general public in how to accelerate the achievement of their personal, professional and financial goals.

Jack Canfield is best known as the co-author of the #1 *New York Times* bestselling *Chicken Soup for the Soul®* book series, which has sold more than 500 million books in 47 languages, including 11 *New York Times* #1 bestsellers. As the CEO of Chicken Soup for the Soul Enterprises he helped grow the *Chicken Soup for the Soul®* brand into a virtual empire of books, children's books, audios, videos, CDs, classroom materials, a syndicated column and a television show, as well as a vigorous program of licensed products that include everything from clothing and board games to nutraceuticals and a successful line of *Chicken Soup for the Pet Lover's Soul®* cat and dog foods.

His other books include *The Success Principles™: How to Get from Where You Are to Where You Want to Be* (recently revised as the 10th Anniversary Edition), *The Success Principles for Teens, The Aladdin Factor, Dare to Win, Heart at Work, The Power of Focus: How to Hit Your Personal, Financial and Business Goals with Absolute Certainty, You've Got to Read This Book, Tapping into Ultimate Success, Jack Canfield's Key to Living the Law of Attraction,* his recent novel, *The Golden Motorcycle Gang: A Story of Transformation* and *The 30-Day Sobriety Solution.*

Jack is a dynamic speaker and was recently inducted into the National Speakers Association's Speakers Hall of Fame. He has appeared on more than 1000 radio and television shows, including Oprah, Montel, Larry King Live, The Today Show, Fox and Friends, and two hour-long PBS Specials devoted exclusively to his work. Jack is also a featured teacher in 12 movies including *The Secret, The Meta-Secret, The Truth, The Keeper of the Keys, Tapping into the Source,* and *The Tapping Solution.* Jack was also honored recently with a documentary that was produced about his life and teachings, *The Soul of Success: The Jack Canfield Story.*

Jack has personally helped hundreds of thousands of people on six different continents become multi-millionaires, business leaders, best-selling authors, leading sales professionals, successful entrepreneurs, and world-class athletes, while at the same time creating balanced, fulfilling and healthy lives.

His corporate clients have included Virgin Records, SONY Pictures, Daimler-Chrysler, Federal Express, GE, Johnson & Johnson, Merrill Lynch, Campbell's Soup, Re/Max, The Million Dollar Forum, The Million Dollar Roundtable, The Young Entrepreneurs Organization, The Young Presidents Organization, the Executive Committee, and the World Business Council.

Jack is the founder of the Transformational Leadership Council and a member of Evolutionary Leaders, two groups devoted to helping create a world that works for everyone.

Jack is a graduate of Harvard, earned his M.Ed. from the University of Massachusetts, and has received three honorary doctorates in psychology and public service. He is married, has three children, two step-children and a grandson.

For more information, visit:
- www.JackCanfield.com

CHAPTER 2

THE STRATEGY OF SUCCESS

BY RICHARD TYLER

"Success is not final; failure is not fatal. It is the courage to continue that counts." This quote is often erroneously attributed to Winston Churchill. I can't tell you who first said it or if it was even said all at once or taken in part from various people. What I can tell you is that successful people work for their success every day, learn from every failure and push through even the darkest times with courage and commitment.

Recent world events have challenged even the most successful businesses. Many who had made it, who found success, have had to start over and rebuild their businesses. Even if their business fails for the moment, their courage and conviction to continue will determine if that failure is temporary or permanent. We all face obstacles. Some would argue that small businesses are always hit harder than larger businesses during challenging times. That may be true; however, even the largest businesses fail. According to a study published in the September 2018 Harvard Business Review, the average lifespan of a U.S. S&P 500 company fell by 80% in the last 80 years (from 67 to 15 years). So big or small, failure is always waiting in the wings for those without the right strategy or those that refuse to stay committed to success.

Of course, I do believe that some people, some businesses, face bigger challenges than others. What I also know to be true is that we all have the *opportunity* to achieve success. Success has *everything* to do with how we meet the challenges between ourselves and our goals.

My philosophy of success is simple: "Your success tomorrow is in direct proportion to your 'Commitment to Excellence' today."

Please don't assume that because I have a philosophy for success that I have always been successful. I started out with little more than motivation to earn an income and admiration for those who were successful. Some of my family members were in the jewelry business, and by that, I mean they did piecework creating fashion jewelry and were paid for each piece they made. My proximity to the industry had given me enough knowledge to sell fashion jewelry face-to-face, door-to-door, but I was not an instant success. From each "No" I received, I learned what I didn't know. Then I found the answers so that next time I knew what to say to improve my odds of getting a "Yes." I made a commitment to learn more and was relentless in doing so. I researched successful businesspeople, read books, recorded myself, and practiced, practiced, practiced.

Many people's primary goal is to build wealth. "Show me how to make the money! What are the shortcuts to making money faster?" They are happy to cut corners to get to profit quicker. Hear me now: shortcuts will never drive lasting success. *What drives lasting success is the commitment to doing the right things repeatedly.* Although there are no shortcuts, nature does provide a scale: on one side is success, on the other is the question, "What price am I willing to pay to achieve it, within moral and ethical boundaries?" Answering the question correctly, for you, opens the door to personal and professional achievement.

A significant number of business owners will be revamping or restarting their businesses this year. They will be rethinking their business models and reflecting on their values, reassessing if what they are committed to is worth the effort. Alongside them are the people reassessing their professional lives and discovering that they want something more or different than they had before. Maybe they love their job, but they have realized that their job is only a fraction of their life. If you apply success principles only to your business life, you will miss out on the profound change you can enact in your entire life.

A few years ago, a woman attended one of my Success Seminars with the intention of learning something for her business growth. She later contacted me to say that she had applied these principles to raising her daughters, and they were flourishing as a result. Our lives don't begin and end at the office, and our success should not be measured only monetarily. I have known many successful businesspersons who did not attain the same level of success in their personal lives. I have also known many people that had successful personal lives but never achieved the same level of success at business. You see, success isn't about one or the other; it is about both! That is what a Life Strategy for Success gives you—both!

To be clear, some success does happen overnight or somewhat by accident. People sometimes resort to unethical behavior or compromise morals for a quicker path to success. Lasting success, however, requires a profound effort coupled with the commitment to sustain it. We will all face challenges. I believe we are all born with the tools necessary to meet those challenges and rise above them. Whether or not we achieve lasting success depends on how we choose to approach the challenges that lie between us and the success we intend to achieve. Most people don't have time to reinvent the wheel before moving forward. They need proven strategies they can begin incorporating today and a commitment to faithfully executing those strategies every day. I have discovered that there are six principles necessary to achieve lasting success in any area a person chooses. I call them the Tyler Learning 6™.

WORK WITH A STRATEGY
Tyler Learning 6™

I have discovered there are six principles necessary to achieving success in whatever it is a person chooses to do:

Step One: Commitment
Commitment is that mental determination to accept only excellence, no matter how difficult, no matter how uncomfortable, and no matter how stressful.

Step Two: Visualization
Visualization is the mental imagining of yourself *as you wish to be.* I have found this is such a critical process, yet so many people do not practice it, and many programs teach nothing about Visualization. It is important to understand that our mind doesn't care whether we're a success or a failure. It will seek to attract to us whatever we condition it to. To condition the mind for success, we must feed it images and thoughts of the way we wish to be, so it can seek out and recognize the paths to obtain the right answers.

Step Three: Application
Application is the physical process of moving from visualization into action.

Step Four: Indoctrination
Indoctrination is the conscious use of your skills. Indoctrination feels awkward and uncomfortable at first, like breaking in a new pair of shoes. In the beginning, you are acutely aware that they are new. You might give up for a day or two and revert to your old, comfortable self. New shoes won't break in themselves; new principles will always feel awkward until you practice them enough that they become part of you.

Step Five: Individualization
Individualization involves converting your knowledge into your beliefs, thinking in original terms, and "walking your talk." When

you first learn the processes that I am talking about, they are initially my thoughts, beliefs, values, and principles about these areas. Through a daily practice of working on these principles yourself, you begin to think of them in original terms, and they are no longer Richard Tyler's beliefs. They become *your* beliefs. Individualization allows you to think in original terms and act as you believe. This is critical so that your mind does not get conflicting messages.

There are many people who will say one thing and do something else. You can't achieve lasting success like that. You can't turn it on part of the time, like a nine to five job. You have to live it, breathe it, and let it become part of you. It's not enough to *commit* to just being successful between the hours of nine and five. Success is a life principle, a belief structure, a set of philosophies, an attitude, and a conviction that is part of you. You are either all in or all out.

Step Six: Review

Review your basics. You have got to go back to the basics frequently to avoid performance slumps, refocus the mind, and re-establish *commitment*. Every day, negative people, negative environments, and negative news pummels you. You are constantly being told the things you can't achieve, and no one, no matter how strong they are, is impervious to this barrage. Little by little, negativity or lack of faith in yourself creeps in, and you don't even recognize it's happening. Your skills begin to erode, your belief structures start to deteriorate, and one day you wake up to find yourself dramatically off course.

Once you have programmed yourself towards a success philosophy, then you must go back and review the basics frequently. You must do the right things that are necessary so you can avoid most setbacks or slowdowns on the road to success. This behavior establishes an environment more likely to experience success. *Review is so critically important* that some people come through my courses again and again to review and revitalize themselves.

27

WHY A STRATEGY IS IMPORTANT

The universe loves order, not chaos. When we adopt a looseness in our attitude, we offend the universe. When we fight that order, we fight success. To create and sustain success, you need three things that help maintain balance and order.

1. Commitment:

Why do I talk so much about commitment? Because without it there is no success of our own making. Think of it like this, our lives are held in place by an invisible force similar to gravity. This force has several names. You may know it as a comfort zone, complacency, or acceptance of our situation. If you want to change, you have to apply positive pressure to move the object, in this case, your life, forward. You wouldn't push a 2-ton boulder with your finger and expect it to move. However, if you committed to moving it and brought the right tools and leveraged those tools toward the effort, it could be moved.

2. Attitude:

People tend to think in terms of, "What do I have and how do I keep it?" This is NOT a successful attitude because it tries to stop the inevitable wheels of change from moving! When you have a Success Dominant Attitude™ you think about "What *don't* I have and how do I get it, within moral and ethical boundaries?" Successful companies and people ultimately fail when they move away from a Success Dominant Attitude™. You cannot wrap yourself around your current situation and protect yourself or your business from change. You must learn to ride the wave of change, or you will get crushed by it. Riding the change wave only happens when you consistently have a Success Dominant Attitude™.

3. Education:

Education comes from the Latin *ēdūcō*, meaning to draw out from within, to lead, to lift up. Therefore, education can mean higher-learning formal education; however, it doesn't have to. Lack of formal education is used as an excuse for lack of success. Thomas Edison, Andrew Carnegie, Henry Ford, and Abraham Lincoln all had little or no formal education, yet each went on to be wildly successful. What they had in common is something all long-term successful people share without regard to their formal education or lack thereof. That is a success philosophy of life-long learning, a never-ending quest for self-improvement. It is possible to look around us and find all the information and support we need to be successful. Books, mentors, seminars, schools are all tools at our disposal. The Secret Key is education and growth must be constant.

Part of education is a review of what we have already learned, as I mentioned in Step 6 of the Tyler Learning 6™. If we don't review, it is easy to start to take shortcuts or forget what was learned.

"Hate the failure, but love the lesson."

Jack Barry, one of the best CEOs I have ever known, is a dear friend of mine. He says, "If we are not growing, we are dying." He is spot-on. If you look in nature, if something is not growing and thriving, it is dying. We experience defining moments in our lives, both personal and professional, that open the door to view where we are and to evaluate where we want to go. At that moment, what will we decide to do? I believe you have to *hate the failure but love the lesson*. There's no lesson if you don't examine the failure. If what you are doing has worked, then how can I improve it? If it failed, what has to change to make it a success?

ONE STRATEGY MULTIPLE APPROACHES

Earlier I spoke of the order and balance the universe demands of us. You can't have balance if your life is two-dimensional, and you put all your energy and growth into only one area. You have to create multiple revenue streams, multiple success streams. Look for multiple ways to put your talent out there. I wrote my first book because I wanted another way to get my ideas out there. It is the same reason I produced my first documentary films, both full-length and short. They were multiple award winners in both categories.

In what ways can you pour more of yourself into the world? You might not love doing certain things that will help you succeed, but there must be a blending of the things you like and dislike for there to be a balance in success.

One phrase I hear people uttering all the time is "work-life balance." I believe that statement is inaccurate. It is all one life – yours. If you compartmentalize work as somehow separate from everything else, it will never work. Make them blend together. They transcend each other. You have to be willing to apply the same commitment, energy, and effort to work and home to achieve lasting success in the life you desire.

A LEGACY OF SUCCESS

The real legacy of a person's success is how many other people's lives he/she has touched in a positive way. The deepest human desire is to feel loved, wanted, needed, and important. Make sure you leave people feeling better for having met you by making a conscious effort to make the world a better place.

Remember, "Your success tomorrow is in direct proportion to your 'Commitment to Excellence®' today."™

About Richard

Richard Tyler, America's Corporate and Entrepreneurial Business Expert™, is recognized as the world's top Sales and Management expert. Richard is the CEO of Richard Tyler International, Inc.®, as well as a diversified family of companies and services.

Richard Tyler is a 3-time Best Selling Author, a 6-time Expy® Award Winner, a 2-time Quilly® Award Winner, a 3-time Editor's Choice Award Winner, and a C-Suite Book Club featured Best-Selling Author. He is a highly acclaimed Professional Speaker, Trainer, and Management Consultant. Richard Tyler is an award-winning Filmmaker and Director. He is the Executive Producer of the documentary *Maximum Achievement - The Brian Tracy Story* as well as the Producer of *The Soul of Success – The Jack Canfield Story*. The films were Emmy Award-nominated and won a Gold TELLY® Award and Bronze TELLY® Award, respectively. Richard is Director and Producer of two Award-winning Short Films, *The Power of Words* and *The Power of Community*. Each film, produced by his film company ***Excellence Edge® Films***, captured top honors by winning seven major national and international awards in the One Reeler Awards and The Global Short Awards. In 2020, *The Power of Community*, which documents the impact of Hurricane Harvey on one family and the resulting community response, earned Richard a Bronze TELLY® Award as Director and a Bronze TELLY® Award for Videography/Cinematography.

Richard Tyler has been inducted into the National Academy of Best-Selling Authors® and the National Association of Experts, Writers, and Speakers.™ Richard was selected as one of America's PremierExperts™ and his philosophies have been featured in *The Wall Street Journal, Forbes* magazine, *Entrepreneur* magazine, *The Business Journals, Sales and Marketing Management* magazine, *Wealth & Finance International* magazine, *Acquisition International* magazine, *Corporate America* magazine, the *Houston Chronicle* as well as in hundreds of articles and interviews. Richard has been seen on FOX, CBS, NBC and ABC television affiliates, Telemundo.com, CNBC.com, Morningstar.com, Moneywatch.com, MarketWatch.com, YahooFinance.com, CNN.com, BBC.com, as well as other major media outlets. Richard is a member of The Business Journals Leadership Trust, an invitation-only organization exclusive to top business leaders.

Richard has earned a worldwide reputation for his powerful educational methods, motivational techniques, and success training. His background in sales, leadership, management, customer service, and quality improvement has allowed him to become one of the world's most sought-after consultants, keynote speakers, and trainers. Richard has authored or co-authored over two dozen books with top experts such as Jack Canfield, Brian Tracy, Mark Victor Hansen, Stephen Covey, Ken Blanchard, Denis Waitley, Dr. Warren Bennis, General Alexander Haig, Alan Keyes, Dr. John Gray, Dr. Robert Schuller, Jack Barry, and many others. Richard shares his success and Excellence philosophies with millions of individuals each year.

As Richard says, **"Remember, your success tomorrow is in direct proportion to your 'Commitment to Excellence®' today.**™**"**

If you would like to learn more about Richard and how he can help you personally or your business, you can visit:
- www.RichardTyler.com
- or call him at +1-713-974-7214.

CHAPTER 3

AN ACCIDENTAL GIFT

BY NORA CHAHBAZI

If you think about your school experience, you may remember moments when you were in 3rd grade, 7th grade, or 11th grade. The teacher called on a student, perhaps it was you, to read a passage aloud. Whether you were a struggling reader or a self-conscious student who agonized over every word, you could relate to the feeling of dread these moments often brought. If you were a student who was listening, you likely knew who the struggling readers in class were and might have cringed even before that anxious child began the first syllable because you knew how torturous it would be for them.

If you were the reader who didn't read well or misread words, flushed cheeks, sweaty palms, and butterflies in the stomach might have been the norm for you. It is also possible that you had fooled everyone. Maybe they all thought you could read because you could memorize a lot of words, or you'd figured out what paragraph would be yours to read and went over it several times in your head before you were called on. However, you knew how difficult it was for you, and feared a potentially humiliating experience was just a moment away.

I was lucky. Reading came easily to me. The same activities I enjoyed in school, like the weekly delivery of the SRA reading skills cart with its color-coded levels and reading cards with questions to answer, felt torturous to my best friend. She, I now know, was confused back then by how reading was supposed to work. Through school, college, and beyond I was unaware that many, actually the majority of people, were not as adept at reading, writing, and spelling as they could be. It wasn't until my own daughter struggled with reading that I started to become aware of this.

The struggle by so many to become highly literate, most commonly the result of a system not equipped to teach reading effectively and efficiently, is an invisible epidemic, a national crisis, and a form of neglect and abuse to those left behind. Ask any adult reader who struggled or continues to struggle with literacy, and most will acknowledge the significant emotional and psychological trauma inflicted on them by a system that was not equipped with the research-based practices to teach them.

Language enhances our lives, and reading is a huge part of that. I want to teach the world to read; it's my mission, my calling. I've dedicated a quarter-century of my life to it. When I started researching reading, I had been a neonatal ICU nurse for a decade. I'd had no formal education or background in education or business. My daughter's struggles with reading and spelling, despite having highly-educated parents, being read to every day from birth, and attending what were deemed excellent schools, led to what I consider my accidental gift.

What has become my life's mission began from a personal need, from pure necessity. Personal need tends to make one exceptionally passionate about something, especially if it involves your child. We first noticed my middle daughter's reading difficulties after we moved back to the United States from Guam in 1996. The small school that my children attended in Guam taught systematic phonics. My oldest daughter picked it up rapidly, and Colleen thrived when instruction consisted of a single letter representing one sound. However, when instruction progressed to learning the complex components of the code and phonics rules that were inconsistent and seemed random to her, she struggled.

She was in first grade when we moved back to Michigan, and by second grade, she was put in the gifted and talented program for her high math scores. This is common, I later learned, with learners who are highly intelligent but sub-literate. Colleen was in the 98th percentile in math on the national Iowa test but a year below grade level in reading on the same test. She was a 'pretend reader'. Her teachers would tell me she was the best reader in the class because she could easily memorize the stories in the reading series. However, she couldn't read a sentence from that same story if it was pulled out, and could not read books she hadn't memorized or seen before. Colleen could spell perfectly on a spelling test because she used rote memory for the test but couldn't spell those words in her writing later that same day.

I keep a sample writing piece of hers from 1997 in my desk drawer as a reminder of why this work I do is so crucial. I remember looking at her horrifically misspelled writing piece at a parent night and thinking, "She's a good speller. What happened? Did my child have a brain injury I'm unaware of?" The picture of dogs was lovely, but I couldn't read what was written because 19 of the 40 words were spelled nothing like they should have been. The teacher brushed off my concern, saying they didn't want to squelch Colleen's creativity and that she'd spell words correctly at some point. That made no sense. When was that supposed to magically happen, and how would she transition to correct spelling without anyone teaching her how to do it? That writing piece was the trigger that started me on this literacy journey and mission.

To start, I researched how to teach reading and spelling. Admittedly, my motivation and enthusiasm were over the top! I read books and research, went to various reading trainings, called schools and asked if I could observe their remediation teaching, and even asked for suggestions in my Christmas letter about reading instruction that worked.

I quickly realized my daughter wasn't the only one struggling. Far from it! Almost every parent I spoke to had at least one child, or several, who struggled. For years, the national reading scores had shown that the majority of 4th and 8th-grade students in our country were not proficient in reading.

When I began researching how to teach reading, I wasn't trying to start a business, let alone a movement. My quest for knowledge was taken to a new level one day when my mom called and told me her 12-year-old twin neighbors, who were in special education, had attended a reading center in Lansing, MI. After 12 hours of instruction, they had made such significant progress that they no longer qualified for special education. My mom gave me the phone number, and I called the center. The owner, a former education professor at a major university, answered the phone herself. That call provided the path to follow to teach my daughter...finally.

This former professor told me that teachers are not taught how to teach reading in college. When she tried to rectify this in her position at the college and was prohibited from doing so, she left her position after having been there three decades and opened her reading center. She also said I needed to immediately get the book, *Why Our Children Can't Read and What We Can Do About It.* I had probably read 50 books on reading instruction by that point and had also read lots of research articles. I immediately ordered the book from the publisher. It came in the mail one afternoon and I read the whole thing before I went to bed that night.

It was the first information I'd come across about how to teach reading that really made sense. I used what was shared in that book and taught my daughter to read in three hours. She went from never having read any book by herself to reading a Bailey

School children's chapter book in one sitting, then telling me all about it! Remediating her spelling took much longer, as she'd been practicing incorrect spelling without being corrected for quite some time.

Parents began asking me to work with their struggling children. These children would come to my house, and I would teach them, on a volunteer basis, with the same instruction I'd used to teach my daughter. Like Colleen, these children made atypical reading gains in a matter of hours. Over this time, I'd been trained in the program described in that life-changing book. I'd also become a teacher trainer and had taught a five-day training to 30 educators. Not much later, my then-husband, a doctor, had a plan to open a wellness center and suggested that I start teaching reading in a room of the building he planned to rent. Before it opened, his wellness center fell through, leaving me with an entire reading center. I named it Ounce of Prevention Reading Center. None of this was planned by me; I have always credited divine intervention for this unique unfolding.

Most days, we had students in our center 8:00-5:00, and people were coming to use it – seemingly from out of the woodwork. I taught them and trained and coached many more teachers with Phono-Graphix, the program I'd been trained in. My instruction and training evolved as I continued to read, learn, teach children and teachers, and explore. I terminated the teacher trainer contract with Phono-Graphix when I realized it really wasn't their training and instruction program I was using anymore; it had evolved into something I'd created with my continuously evolving knowledge and practice.

The week after I gave up their system, a foundation offered to fund any teacher in their county who wanted to be trained by me over the next three years. However, I didn't have a teacher training anymore! Thus, EBLI was born.[*] As I continued to teach and coach teachers, I came to know that the professor who led me to the solution for Colleen was right: teachers are not

---

[*] Evidence-Based Literacy Instruction

taught how to teach reading in college. Studies of Colleges of Education confirm this and countless teachers I'd trained told me they realized this and were very distraught by it. I began to change more of my focus from our reading center, with parents paying to remediate their children who hadn't been taught in school, to teaching educators to ensure they possessed effective, efficient, research-based instruction to teach their students. I love teaching children, but really, teaching the teachers and providing them that bridge from the research to practice is what was most desperately needed.

While we have trained thousands and thousands of educators and others in EBLI, we have never had a sales plan or people whose job was to sell EBLI. Word of mouth advertising has been the impetus for EBLI's growth and it spread to educators and homeschoolers from around the country and the world. When administrators or educators are looking to change and are ready to refine their instruction, they tend to find EBLI. We've become adept at interacting with schools and districts to help them shift from instructional practices that leave many students sub-literate or reading below/well below their potential, to practices that assist them in getting 95-100% of their students proficient in reading, spelling, and writing.

There have been many times that I've thought about how returning to nursing would be a much more secure and easy path than this literacy mission. However, I've never seriously considered it because this literacy work is what I was put on this earth to do. Based on EBLI's trajectory, it feels very much that this path has been predestined or fated. I really am an accidental entrepreneur. I have become conditioned to being open to the challenges that present themselves and thinking outside the box to address them. The recent pandemic was no exception. We had been developing an online teacher training and student learning system for several years. The Covid-19 pandemic created an opportunity to accelerate its creation, and provide educators with virtual training, and especially student instruction that worked well virtually or in a hybrid setting.

Financially we struggled like so many other businesses, but 2020 was a really good year for us in some unexpected ways. When schools closed with the pandemic, parents and teachers alike were at a loss of how to get reading instruction to the children in younger grades. One morning I woke up with the idea to offer free instruction to groups of K, 1st, and 2nd, and older students online. Though I'd never done that before, we were able to create it and get it out to the world.

Just two weeks after children had been sent home, I taught the first lessons and continued to do so twice a week for eight weeks. Almost 4000 families from around the world signed up, and we'd have over 100 little ones attend live sessions of the interactive lessons! Parents raved about their children's gains and engagement with the lessons, and teachers would recommend them to all their students' families. One 3rd grader in Malaysia begged her mom to stay up to attend live. Her lessons were held at midnight in their time zone! It was great fun to teach these lessons and opened my eyes to what is possible with online instruction direct to large numbers of young children.

Opportunities have always presented themselves to me and grown the EBLI mission in unusual ways. I've almost come to expect it. I call those opportunities "accidental gifts" because typically, I wasn't pursuing them and had no idea how they would change EBLI or my life. My struggle to teach my own child to read evolved into a desire to achieve 95-100% reading proficiency in the United States. An interview for "50 in 52" about my program was discovered by someone at Oprah radio--this was before you could find just about anything on social media--and led to Maya Angelou interviewing me for Oprah's program.

The most recent accidental gift to present itself is my collaboration with The John Corcoran Foundation and DNAFilms to produce a documentary on the current literacy/ sub-literacy crisis as well as how to rectify it. John Corcoran is the author of *The Teacher Who Couldn't Read* and *The Reading Gap*, and Nick Nanton is the Emmy award-winning director and producer of this upcoming literacy documentary film. John and I have a shared mission to remove the stigma of sub-literacy and banish the excuses for why children and adults can't read. "They can't read because they're immigrants. They can't read because their parents work too much. They can't read because their parents work too little. They can't read because their brain is wired differently."

The truth is, they can't read because they haven't been taught... yet. It is time to ensure all learners are effectively taught and that every teacher is equipped to teach every child (and adult) to read, write, and spell to their highest potential. It is my intention that my accidental gift will serve to assist in solving countless problems that stem from literacy difficulties, from the emotional pain and suffering of each of the millions who are affected, to the extensive societal woes that result from the majority of citizens lacking proficient levels of literacy.

About Nora

Nora Chahbazi is the Founder and Creator of Evidence-Based Literacy Instruction (EBLI). She is a Master Teacher Trainer and Teacher Coach. Nora's EBLI Training requires a substantial paradigm shift for the majority of educators, and Nora specializes in holding space for and guiding teachers through the shift in an honest and respectful manner.

Nora's literacy journey began in 1997 when her 2nd-grade daughter scored at the 98th percentile on the Iowa test for math – but on the same test, she was reading a year below grade level. As a concerned parent, Nora turned to the school for answers but didn't receive help. After launching into a full investigation, Nora found the evidence-aligned instructional processes that she needed to help her child outside of the school. Armed with the tools she'd discovered, Nora taught her daughter to read in three hours. She then began teaching other learners in her home, which eventually led to the opening of Ounce of Prevention Reading Center in 1999 and the creation of EBLI in 2003.

Nora's EBLI Training is built upon the Science of Reading, and Nora is an esteemed expert in the Science of Reading community. She is the author of a bi-weekly blog and host of monthly webinars that aim to educate the public about the most current, effective, and efficient literacy research and instruction. Her blog posts and webinars are read, watched, and shared by thousands of educators and parents across the world.

A dynamic speaker, Nora has been asked to present at countless school districts and many education conferences, including MAPSA, MASSP, ACT, LATA, and The Reading League. She has been interviewed by several exceptional individuals, including Maya Angelou, Jack Canfield, Carolyn Clifford, Nick Nanton, Emily Hanford, and John Corcoran.

In addition to EBLI Training, Nora has also created a collection of resources for student instruction, including four EBLI Apps, online non-fiction read alouds, and online student lessons.

Through training thousands of educators and teaching hundreds of thousands of students, Nora has proven that with science-based, effective, efficient instruction, unnecessary suffering can be eradicated, and every learner is capable of reading, writing, and spelling to their highest potential. Her mission is to teach the world to read.

Connect with Nora at:
- Website: www.ebli.com
- Facebook: www.facebook.com/EBLIreads
- Email: info@ebli.com

CHAPTER 4

BUILDING RELATIONSHIPS AND RESULTS

BY SABRINA WALKER HERNANDEZ

"The toilet is clogged, and I just can't do it." That is the first thing I hear walking into the office. I am a successful nonprofit executive. I grew my budget from $750,000 to $2.5 million in the third poorest county in the U.S.A. I was stressed out, constantly putting out fires, and had no work-life balance.

One morning I went to work early. I had my time all planned out. I was going to prepare for a major foundation meeting. But when I walked in, one of two staff members that arrived in the morning was having a major meltdown. She greets me with tears in her eyes, saying the toilet is clogged, and I just can't do it. Now normal business folks would say, just call maintenance. But you, my nonprofit brothers and sisters, you already know the deal... there was no money in the budget for hiring maintenance staff!

So, I am looking at her like, OK, and....?

My leadership mantra comes to mind: "I will never ask a staff member to do something too small or gross (in this case) that I am not willing to do myself." So, I rolled up my sleeves, put on some gloves, and marched into the restroom. Yep, it was the worst-case scenario—a combination of toilet paper and excrement. And I thought to myself, this is some bull crap (no pun intended)! But, remembering my mantra, I got the job done.

Afterward, I checked on the staff, prepared for my meeting, and later that afternoon, boarded a private plane to give a major grant pitch. Yep, I managed to clean a nasty, stopped-up toilet bowl and boarded a nice private plane, all in one day. During all this, I have been struggling, but no one even knew. I had become the queen of "fake it, till you make it" and had the crown to prove it. We were currently in the middle of a $12 million capital campaign, and I am thrilled to say that we got that major grant. Whew!

A couple of years after that, I heard the three scariest words in the English language. YOU HAVE CANCER! Oh, and by the way, not just one cancer... but two, at the same time – Non-Hodgkin's Lymphoma and Multiple Myeloma. I have always been an overachiever, but this took the cake. I did not know you could get two cancers at the same time, but even rarer to get the two I had. I am a part of the lucky one percent!

Like most people, you start examining your lifestyle—obesity, stress levels, food, etc. My husband was convinced it was the stress of my job. So, on one of my weak days, I made a promise to him that I would retire. Since that day, "I love what I do, I love what I do" was on repeat in my head. I have so much knowledge and experience that can help others, and I loved getting up every day to make the world a better place through my work.

I wanted to help others stop the exhausting fundraising grind without adding another time-sucking task to their to-do list. I went to work and, guess what created a way? Hence, the brainchild, *Supporting World Hope*, was developed.

Through my past experiences, I was the stressed out, no work-life balance, constantly-putting-out-fires Executive. I was successful. I grew my budget from $750,000 to $2.5 million in the third poorest county in the U.S.A., and I completed a $12 million capital campaign in a recession and even hired maintenance and janitorial staff! So, I know what it is like to overcome obstacles in my personal life and my work.

I use the B.U.I.L.D. approach to building relationships to overcome my fundraising obstacles. What I know is that a nonprofit business or any business can overcome its revenue obstacle by building good relationships.

RELATIONSHIP + RESULTS = RECURRING REVENUE

The B.U.I.L.D. ACRONYM
> **B – Brand Yourself**
> **U – Unleash Your Potential**
> **I – Inspire Those Around You**
> **L – Leverage Your Connections**
> **D – Discover Their Story**

I. BRAND YOURSELF

—A good business reputation goes hand in hand with maintaining good relationships. Those with a bad reputation will have a difficult time connecting with other businesses and contacts. Think about it...who wants to be associated with someone with a tarnished name and image? A boss once told me your reputation needs to be so good that if someone talks negatively about you, no one believes them, and, in fact, it brings the "bone carrier's" character into question.

When you are networking, you automatically become the face of your organization. You are effectively representing them so that your organization will be immediately identifiable with you. Make a good first impression, but make it a point to make a good impression every single time. If you have a resting b*tch face. Smile. Do not drive them away by looking gloomy or depressed. That certainly will not get you anywhere!

(i). **Build trust:** *Never* take advantage of people. Don't even let them think that you'd do so. It's the quickest way to ruin a relationship and build a bad reputation that can harm other relationships too. The key to building trust is being honest. When you are willing to forego your interests to help someone else, they know they can rely on you. Always think about how you can help people in your network. They're far more likely to return a favor than they are to go out of their way for you, especially early in your relationship.

(ii). **Show an interest in others:** Pretentious people who talk about themselves all the time don't get far. Smart people know that an early step to gaining respect and building a relationship is to show interest in other people. Listen to what people have to say and show a sincere interest in them. Ask questions about their job and kids. Keep track of what they've brought up in the past and follow up with them. Everyone is impressed when someone shows they've taken the time to remember their stories. For my introverts, you excel at this. You listen and retain information. So, focus on this as your strength and not a weakness during networking.

(iii). **Work hard:** People want to invest in success and someone who is going to provide results. You might need to show them that you can deliver before you can expect them to have your back or put in a good word for you. When someone asks for something, give a little more. My motto is under-promise and over-deliver. Deliver early and take the initiative to help in ways you weren't asked. It takes effort to build relationships. You might have to be the first one to do a favor.

Now, here are the no-no's in Branding yourself:

1. Failing to be consistent: In all relationships, people deserve to know that your good intentions are genuine. If you are good to someone good to you, but they see you failing to treat others the same way, they will question your motives. They may think you are sucking

up or being deceptive. *Treating everyone you meet the same helps you come across as sincere and genuine.*

2. <u>Failing to admit your mistakes:</u> Part of developing trust is showing that you know how to be accountable. *If you mess up, fess up!* People understand that mistakes are made, but lying about them can cause permanent damage to your relationships.

3. <u>Not being reliable:</u> Just like when businesses deceivingly change their policies or don't meet obligations, you can offend someone when you're not reliable. Don't miss meetings, and don't 'flake' on promises. These mistakes can cost your relationships significantly. *Your value is only as good as your word.*

4. <u>Not being careful what you say:</u> Everyone makes mistakes in conversation. A simple slip of the tongue can cost you a lot in the long run. I have seen people drink a little too much at events and start saying things they later regret. No matter where you are or who you are with, you are representing yourself, so try to be professional. *Remember, if you speak poorly about people behind their backs to someone, that person will be wary that you may do the same to them.*

5. <u>Surrounding yourself with untrustworthy people:</u> You're going to be judged by the company you keep. *If your friends or business contacts have shady reputations or histories of dishonesty, then you're building that same reputation for yourself.*

II. UNLEASH YOUR POTENTIAL

—We are all busy people. It's one thing to realize you need to act and devote some time to nurturing relationships and another thing to do it. You must be intentional about building relationships by getting out of the office. Often you don't know what people you need to connect with. If you did, connecting with them would be as easy as shooting off a quick email.

But in a lot of cases, it's the unexpected people who will add to your network. Build new relationships by diversifying your networks. Force yourself to go beyond people in your immediate circle and those you know well. Challenge yourself to nurture a real relationship with at least one potential donor, client, supplier, and competitor. The next step is to reach out to people from unrelated organizations, such as the media and government.

Also, spend time with your most important donors or customers, your most productive employees, and leaders who can make the most difference to your organization. These relationships will generate returns in the immediate future and the long term. You must aim to make long-lasting connections that will remain for a very long time.

So, act, identify 20 people who can help you move your organization forward. Put them on a list and block time in your calendar to reach out and then schedule meetups with them. This could be a formal meeting, coffee appointment, or going out for a happy hour.

Don't get overwhelmed. Break those 20 people down into small manageable chunks. Change the conversation in your head. Connect with four people per quarter.

By reaching out, you are developing a trusting relationship. Thank them for what they did for you in the past, see how they are doing, and make sure they haven't forgotten you.

III. INSPIRE THOSE AROUND YOU

—Give as much as you expect to get from every relationship. Effective relationships in business require reciprocity – not a one-way, half-hearted effort. Offer and deliver help, connect people, or share industry or nonprofit-sector information. Only then will you feel satisfied and find others willing to respond when you need help.

IV. LEVERAGE YOUR CONNECTIONS

—John Maxwell once said: "Your network is your net worth." Networking is the key to building successful relationships, and you have many options available to you. I serve in my community and attend as many mixers and nonprofit events as I can to meet new contacts.

Be strategic about networking. The goal is to make a lasting impression on a handful of contacts. A mentor once advised me that the best goal at a networking event is to get *just one good* business card. That doesn't mean turning away everyone else you meet because you don't know which contacts are going to be the most promising. Follow up with anyone with whom you may have a quality relationship later. Just don't overwhelm yourself trying to keep up with too many new people.

Remember, networking doesn't have to be this formal. You can strike up a friendly conversation with someone at the gym. I once received a lead from someone I met at a friend's birthday party. If you are engaging with other people, you are actively networking.

V. DISCOVER THEIR STORY

—When you're trying to get a person to trust you, you must work for it because they are under no obligation to trust you. You need to form a connection through personalization, just like with marketing. Find out what you have in common, learn about their hobbies, families, interests without seeming nosy.

So, get out there, get up from the desk! You're missing out on a wonderful opportunity to grow professionally while tapping into the most basic human need—belonging and friendship.

About Sabrina

Sabrina Walker Hernandez is a certified consultant, coach, and facilitator that helps small nonprofit Staff and Boards build relationships that convert into more donations. Being brought up in a home by a missionary who was constantly giving back to the church and the community, Sabrina naturally gravitated to the nonprofit world. Sabrina began her "official" nonprofit career as an intern in 1996. In 1998, she found her home with the Boys & Girls Clubs, where she served for 20 years and worked in the capacity of direct services, operations, and executive leadership.

Sabrina has a reputation for transformational leadership through staffing and mission alignment, fundraising, expanding programming, and community partnerships. One of Sabrina's greatest successes is that she increased operation revenue from $750,000 to $2.5 million over an 8-year period. She was also responsible for planning, operating, and completing a $12-million comprehensive capital campaign and establishing a $500,000 endowment in the third poorest county in the United States. With this knowledge, she has helped her clients gain confidence in fundraising, engage their board in fundraising, and build fundraising systems. She has worked with a variety of nonprofits – from startups to those with a $4-million budget.

Sabrina understands that nonprofits enrich our world and works in partnership with her clients to build stronger nonprofit businesses. Her philosophy is "nonprofits can achieve long-term success when they have effective leaders, sound strategies, and diversified resources. Ultimately, this empowers them to fully sustain their mission and impact – in the arts, education, health and human services, medical research, conservation, animal protection, and communities of faith."

Sabrina holds a Certification in Nonprofit Management from Harvard Business School, a Master of Public Administration from the University of Texas—RGV, and a Management Advanced Leadership Certification from the Strom Thurmond Leadership Institute from Clemson University. She is the President and C.E.O. of Supporting World Hope, a nonprofit consulting agency specializing in management, fundraising, and leadership. She is a certified Master National Trainer for Boys & Girls Clubs of America and certified in David P. Weikart Methods Training of the Trainer. Sabrina has trained and facilitated workshops with thousands of nonprofit professionals across the country.

She is the recipient of numerous recognitions in the nonprofit world, but the one of which she is most proud of is being selected by the C.E.O. of Boys & Girls Clubs of America for serving as an inspiration and as a catalyst, resulting in transformational change of an organization with the Boys and Girls Clubs Movement.

Sabrina is an active community leader and volunteer in Edinburg, Texas, where she is based. Because of her service, she has been inducted into the BorderFest Rio Grande Valley Walk of Fame, been named a Rotary Rotarian of the Year, and a Paul Harris Fellow twice. She has also been the recipient of the Golden Fire Hydrant from the Edinburg Volunteer Fire Department.

You can connect with Sabrina at:
- Email: sabrina@supportingworldhope.com
- LinkedIn: https://www.linkedin.com/in/sabrinawalkerhernandez/
- Website: www.supportingworldhope.com
- Facebook: https://www.facebook.com/supportingworldhope
- Instagram: https://www.instagram.com/the_nonprofitexpert

CHAPTER 5

GOING AFTER WHAT YOU WANT

CHANGING YOUR MINDSET AND SHOWING UP FOR YOURSELF

BY DANIEL MANGENA

There is so much important work we can do to change our life and bring forth success and prosperity. Often we don't realize how our own minds lay the blueprint for our own possibilities; how our history, energy, memories, and intentions all impact our lives.

What if I told you there are changes you could make right now that would bring success you only have dreamed of? In this chapter, I'll outline tips for clearer vision and how to change your thinking process. We'll discuss limiting beliefs, reframing negative to positive thoughts, and checking in with your emotions as well as your body.

But to begin, we must first understand how powerful the mind is, and how much our own thoughts can be the very thing blocking us from our own success. I'm referring to limiting beliefs and how self-sabotage and energetic fear may be brimming below the surface, interrupting us from our best selves.

WHAT ARE LIMITING BELIEFS?
(What's keeping you from your achievements?)

You've probably heard of concepts like imposter syndrome, negative self-talk, and self-sabotage. What they have in common is how they are occurrences in our inner selves that tell us what we're not worthy of. Unfortunately, they dominate our internal narrative and impact our sense of self-worth. For imposter syndrome, maybe we see our shortcomings as reasons for not trying to push up for a promotion at work. And of course, both negative self-talk and self-sabotage are toxic ways of keeping ourselves from succeeding. All of these examples are limiting beliefs. Simply put, limiting beliefs are damaging stories we tell ourselves that stand in our own way. Left unchecked, they become self-fulfilling prophecies.

What if these thoughts could be converted to positive outcomes? Your beliefs, emotions, and intentions are capable of giving you everything you need to succeed. You see, there are cyclical patterns that constrict our ability to expand and adapt. As emotional beings, we are often operating from a place of negative habits, fear, and even over-reactivity. So often our decision-making process is reactive – it's based on fears and emotions. Even self-sabotage can take many forms; so often I talk to people who are so hungry for success, and yet they continue to engage in actions (for example, taking on too much or too little) that keep them from achieving their own goals.

Take myself for example. My young adult life was defined by examples of falling short. I have a vivid memory watching my initial successes fall away just because I hadn't yet acknowledged the power support in my life. I can directly tie my financial losses of my early twenties to not having the experience that can be hired through proper mentorship and support. Today, I acknowledge how important my own powerful mind, and the support of others, have been in my many successes. And my intent is to guide and help others achieve their prosperity with these powerful frameworks.

CLEARING EXERCISES

So often what we experience as burn out, imposter syndrome, and even professional recklessness can actually be signs that you are afraid to succeed. I invite you to clear your trauma to help you pave the way to success. What is clearing? One way to look at it is as a personal process of getting present and back to love. As with most personal growth, you must choose your clearing toolbox with knowledge and understanding of yourself in mind.

I recommend this to anyone looking for additional ways to understand their mind and emotions. For the purpose of this chapter, I'll share a few that complement "success." Start with these examples to identify what might work for you, and continue to explore further options. For further learning, visit my website and the Clearing Toolkit – within those pages I give an "encyclopedic" approach to opportunities and philosophies, inviting you to find the one(s) that resonate(s) deepest for you.

Here are five clearing exercises to use as starting points:

1. *Change your inputs*: Stop reading the papers and watching the news. Curate your social media feed or even consider coming off social media for a while (I did it for 12 months and am still alive). What TV shows are you watching? What book are you reading right now? How are these things making you feel? Switch your sensory inputs to ones that serve your joy.

2. *Mind your language*: Speak in absolutes and not possibilities (i.e., use "I will" or "I am" and lose the "might" and most definitely the "can't"). Lose any of the words you use that are loaded with disempowerment.

3. *Talk it out* (and not in): Therapy is a powerful tool when properly employed. Approach it from a state of empowerment. Use therapy as an opportunity to explore what must be healed in a safe and supported space. Therapy is also a space to get the "junk" off your chest. It is better out than in, but

let it out to keep it out! This is about clearing after all, not staying in (the energy of) the person, place or thing that is holding you back.

4. *Breathing work*: There are a number of different types of breathing exercises available that can be explored to change your mood, increase your energy and even heal your body. I personally practice Kundalini yoga, but there are many tools out there that can shift you in a matter of minutes.

5. *Change your physiology* (get more exercise): Get up, move your body, straighten your back and warm your muscles – physiological changes have a proven effect on your mood. Running and other forms of exercise release endorphins into the bloodstream. These are scientifically proven to give you the space to make new choices and seek opportunities.

The next time you catch yourself feeling stuck, afraid, or even just wondering what's next, I invite you to ask yourself this question: what is the thing you're not looking at? What are your blockers? What are you afraid of? You may just find that the thing you're not looking at is the very thing holding you back. Don't let your limiting beliefs keep you from your achievements. Your prosperity and success are possible!

One important thing to note about mindset and beliefs are that your thoughts and emotions are tethered to your physical realities, too. This is why exercise, breath work, yoga, and other modes of self-care all count as clearing exercises, too. Consider that mindset doesn't always address our individual physical realities. Therefore, it's important to pay close attention to your body for clues and make adjustments where needed. Ask yourself: What is my body saying? Do I have the physical, mental, and emotional stamina for change right now? And if so, do I know what my next actions need to be? ...More on questions to ask yourself below.

Ultimately, you will need to show up differently to get a different outcome. And finally, if you don't find inspiration or positivity from your thoughts, change the station.

CHANGE YOUR THINKING PROCESS

Our narrative/stories hold our mental identity together – what I believe is possible comes from within. And we are defined by our intention. However many of us acknowledge that a healthy mind has the power to dramatically change your life for the positive.

A woman I coached a few years ago was afraid to start her own business, until she realized why: she was afraid that she might not succeed, and that she would be viewed as a failure by her family. That fear held her back from even trying, staying in a job that she hated, the misery of which rippled into her relationships and even had impacts on her health. But once she addressed the fear, she was able to open her desire to live life on her terms, and to go for her dream business, knowing that she was supported and had everything to gain by bringing her gifts to the world. We worked on the energy and mindset that she was bringing to the business, and supported her in getting a team of experts to be a part of her project, which ended up being a resounding success.

Now, there are a few ways to approach this shift in our mindset. Of course, switching the scripts (from negative to positive) is a solid way to start. Pay attention to the way you talk about opportunities and make a note where you find yourself stuck.

INTRODUCING: THE FLOW FUNNEL

I first shared the flow funnel of this model and its relationship to the *Beyond Intention* paradigm in my Micro2Millions group coaching program. It was there, in relation to creating financial abundance, that I saw how well this idea could support our intentions and connect us to prosperity. The four steps of the Flow Funnel are: Intention, Feeling, Believing, and Acting. Read on to understand how this framework can support you and your future successes.

Rituals and habits ultimately determine how effective you are in your daily life. Like training for a marathon, change doesn't happen overnight, but honoring a process such as the flow funnel gives you the framework to make incremental change, and hold yourself accountable. Using a framework like the Flow Funnel helps us connect with our bodies and minds, and channel the energy we need to be successful into our day-to-day. Follow these four steps from intention-setting to activation, and allow yourself to experience a deliberate journey of change.

The Flow Funnel invites us to take action with each incremental step:

1. INTENDING: Focus, then choose a thought.

2. FEELING: Use your heart to feel the thought/intention. Connect to the feelings of the experience that are aligned to the outcome of the intention you have chosen to experience.

3. BELIEVING: See or mentally rehearse in your mind's eye the possibility of the thought/intention. What you are doing is mentally observing the occurrence or fruition of the intention before you experience it.

4. ACTING: Act in accordance with your beliefs with regard to how you must come to the experience. This creates alignment with your inner world. You achieve this by acting as if the intention has already manifested. To act as such is to live in a state of positive expectation—it's to have gratitude for the outcome of the potential. Now you simply need to connect to that intention, as opposed to living in fear or lack that it will not come to be (those limiting thoughts I mentioned earlier in this chapter).

Intend, Feel, Believe, Act...then Experience. Use the flow funnel to work on yourself and channel your success.

SHOWING UP FOR YOUR OWN
DESIGNATED PRACTICE

If you're reading this book you might be hoping for quick answers, but we all know that fulfilling our destinies isn't something that can happen overnight. Changing your thinking process and making positive changes in your life begins with effort. Plan to show up for your own success by committing actual time and energy to designated practice. Begin in ways that feel actionable and can be a part of your daily life. One great way to begin is by scheduling check-ins with yourself. Think of this as a time for you to answer questions, set intentions, and commit to holding yourself accountable.

For example, I have four daily check-ins with myself. I begin with a morning practice and alignment opportunity very early. Throughout the day I come back to those intentions by connecting with myself, both with check-ins and meditation. The cadence that works for me is to do so every 4-5 hours. By the time my day winds down in the evening, I spend some time journaling, doing yoga, or meditating.

There are two hard parts of establishing your own designated practice:

- *The first is committing to the act.* Set the intention in terms that work for you but know that the work that needs to be done will not happen all on its own. Our brains like to know what's coming: when you commit to a practice, make it "real" by holding time in your daily ledger or planner, or setting a recurring alarm on your phone, or even by setting a calendar task or event. When you receive a notification that reminds you, don't put it off – you're only putting yourself and your success off when you do.

- *The second hard part is, of course, being present.* Our minds are always wandering, remembering things we need to do, replaying a conversation, or even daydreaming. Curbing distracting thoughts takes dedication and perseverance, but is very important as part of the daily check-ins and your own practice is concerned. For me, I don't give my mind a chance to wander unaccompanied without an agenda or intention – I sometimes make the analogy that my mind is a child and I don't want to leave him unsupervised. This helps me keep my intentions and create structure and discipline – don't disrupt the pattern, and focus on the success you want.

One great way to stay focused is to ask yourself questions. It's important to "interrupt" yourself (including disruption of bad habits, self-talk, disorganized or distracted thinking, etc.), to steer yourself and your practice towards success.

Here are some of the kinds of questions you may ask yourself during your daily check-ins:

- What am I feeling?
- Am I happy?
- What am I grateful for?
- What does my body need?
- Where might my belief systems keep me from success?

IN CONCLUSION

To be successful in different areas of life, you need to allow yourself to access the resources it takes to be prosperous. In this chapter, we've talked about the connection between your mind and body: how things like the way we talk to ourselves and others, how we connect with our physical selves, and how our thinking processes all are factors that can limit or empower us. I've described The Flow Funnel and clearing exercises (more information on these and more are available on my website). Make a conscious effort to use them in your day-to-day, including by journaling or list-making. Come back to the page to see how your intentions may have been positively impacted by clearing over time.

My final suggestion to you is this: treat each aspect of your being with the care and nourishment that it needs. I believe each of these has the ability to empower each of you to instigate more positive changes in your life, and ultimately, to greater successes.

The next step is up to you...

About Daniel

After receiving a late diagnosis of Asperger's and experiencing what can only be described as life-shattering trauma at the age of just 20, Daniel Mangena spent the next seven years struggling to keep these revelations and events from spilling into every area of his life. As a result of his struggles, Daniel built a simple, four-step system called the *Beyond Intention* Paradigm.

Initially built as a lifeline grappling with suicidal thoughts, Beyond Intention was born, transforming Daniel's life from misery to celebration. Through his own struggles, Daniel found a path to lasting joy and purpose, and he wants nothing more than to share the tools that saved his life. To that end, he lives by this mission statement: "To Spearhead an evolutionary uplift in universal consciousness by awakening people to the importance of their unique role. This that is already encoded in them by way of a deep and often ignored or undervalued passion defined as their Dream."

Through his motivational speech, Daniel shares his vision of empowerment and joy. The books he has authored, his *Do it With Dan* podcast series (which is available on all major platforms, regular blogs, published articles and worldwide workshops), have all helped thousands across the globe. His prolific work recently earned him a spot in *The Wall Street Journal* as a "Master of Success."

Daniel Mangena's work has been seen on *The Wall Street Journal*, *Forbes*, *The Today Show* website and on ABC, NBC, CBS & FOX networks.

CHAPTER 6

YOUR THREE KEYS TO SUCCESS
YOUR STORY - YOUR MINDSET YOUR WHY

BY ELLIE D. SHEFI

In 2012, I got a call from a friend of mine. His troubled teenage niece, "Jessie" (not her real name), had just come to live with him, was acting out, was getting straight Fs, and was close to flunking out of high school. He knew that I mentored teenagers and asked me if I could help Jessie get back on track. "She's a smart kid," he told me, "But she's having difficulty adjusting to school. She's not used to having a schedule, or fulfilling others' expectations, or having to go to class. She's never had someone care that she does her homework, and she's not used to having consequences if she doesn't perform. She's just not putting in the work, and I'm afraid she's going to fail and drop out. No one's ever believed in her or refused to let her give up. Do you think you can get through to her?"

Whenever I hear about teenagers or adults giving up on themselves, it makes me sad. But, unfortunately, that kind of limiting, self-sabotaging, and defeatist attitude is all too common.

In my decades of teaching, tutoring, coaching, and mentoring young people, women, entrepreneurs, authors, and speakers, I've observed that many people give up because they've gotten awfully good at telling themselves *why* they can't do something instead of *how* they might succeed. They believe the lies they tell themselves and the lies they've heard from others about their lack of abilities and lack of prospects. Even when they *desire* to succeed, they are still held back by the negative voices in their heads.

Yet these are capable people, with gifts to share and valuable contributions to make to the world. Why are they holding themselves back or allowing themselves to be held back by their circumstances? Why do they stay stuck while other people thrive?

Growing up, I had every possible reason for being held back by my circumstances. My family didn't have money for extras, so we would collect aluminum cans and newspapers from the garbage and take them to the recycling center to get some money. We would eat frozen burritos and frozen dinners that we'd get on sale 10 for $1.00 and we'd buy our clothes at the 99¢ store.

I survived abuse, rape, domestic violence, homelessness, and cancer. I've been called a "medical miracle" by doctors who, time and time again, told me I would soon be dead. But, from a young age, I discovered and studied some of the best teachers in personal development. And I was fortunate to have learned from them the power that is derived from reframing your perspective, choosing empowering meanings, and remembering that life happens *for* you, not *to* you. I also learned from them the pivotal nature of gratitude and how gratitude can transform even the most difficult circumstances. These principles have been my guiding force, and today I use them to help others.

I managed to find the strength within me to overcome poverty, escape an abusive relationship, find the right doctors to help me heal, and, ultimately, create a successful life as an attorney, entrepreneur, award-winning author, featured speaker, strategist, teacher, trainer, mentor, and coach. I learned how to find my voice, stand in my power, and own who I am. And I believe that everyone has within them the power to do the same.

While it may look and feel different to each of us, success in any form requires mastery of three important principles:

1. The story you tell yourself.
2. The mindset you hold.
3. The power of your why.

1. Your Story Matters. Does It Empower You Or Imprison You?

It's my life's mission to help people to break free of the stories that society, our parents, our experiences, and our insecurities tell us. I empower my clients with the tools and strategies they need to define for themselves who they are, what they stand for, and what's important to them so they can become the architect of their lives. They learn to see through the stories they have been telling themselves so they can take control and write new stories that represent their authentic, empowered selves.

I used this process with Jessie. I quickly discovered that she was buying into some extremely negative stories about herself and her potential. No one had ever told Jessie that she was smart or capable. Instead, the adults in her life warned her that she would turn out like her father (who was in jail) or her mother (who was on drugs). And the kids she hung out with reinforced the story that it wasn't worth putting in the effort to do well in school because it wouldn't get them anywhere in "real life."

For the rest of the school year, Jessie and I worked to change her story about herself. With reassurance that she could do the work and that she was smart and resourceful, she learned to think critically and to problem solve. Her self-esteem and confidence bloomed. She recognized the power of incremental progress and learned to celebrate every success. Over time, she began to fully accept that opportunities would come her way if she held herself accountable. Together, her uncle and I assured her, "You can be anyone and do anything you want in life. It doesn't matter what your parents' story is—their story is not your story. What do you want your story to be?"

How you define yourself determines what you consider yourself capable of doing and achieving. I believe that you are neither defined by nor confined by your circumstances. You can rise above and choose for yourself what your life will be. But it starts with your story.

What story do you tell yourself? When you look at your life, are you a victim or a victor? Are you simply repeating the put-downs, limiting beliefs, and negative comments you've heard from parents, siblings, significant others, and people in class or at work? Or are you telling a story that demonstrates your power, your purpose, and your ability to overcome whatever challenges you encounter?

Words have power. And too often, we become victims of the stories that we tell ourselves or that we absorb from those around us. Some of the most important work you can do is to take control of the story you tell yourself, because your story can either empower you or imprison you. But when you define for yourself who you are and what you stand for, you create a new story. And when you own your story and tell it authentically, it will become your vehicle for victory.

2. Do You Have an Impervious Mindset?

From the time I was ten years old, I learned from reading personal development books and listening to audios that mindset was everything. The lesson that you have to control your mind at every moment in order to find a way out of your circumstances was my lifesaver. No matter how bad my circumstances, I discovered that with an impervious mindset, I was unstoppable.

One of the best ways to build an impervious mindset is by working with a mentor or a coach. Over the time that Jessie and I met, her mindset got stronger. Each time she said, "I can't do this; it's too hard," I would counter with, "You can do this, and you're worth it. You're strong enough and smart enough to handle anything. How can you look at this in a different way so that it makes sense to you?" Eventually, I didn't have to say that anymore because she believed it herself. I will never forget the immense pride I felt the first time she said, "I can do it; just give me a minute to figure it out."

As we worked together, Jessie's confidence in herself and her abilities grew, and she began to develop an impervious mind. She started thinking and acting differently. Her grades went up, and her sense of what was possible for her future expanded dramatically. From that troubled teenage girl who quickly and frequently said, "I can't," she became a vibrant, powerful, happy young woman who graduated from high school with a 4.0 grade point average, who attended college, and who, in fact, graduated from college also with a 4.0 grade point average. Today, she is a successful professional and a mother.

I love mentoring underserved young people like Jessie because I was one of them. I understand how their environment—one of poverty, high unemployment, and limited resources—can undermine their mindset. Surrounded by others with low expectations hampers any of their potential visions for a different kind of future. But with mentoring, these young people can learn to stand guard at the gate of their mind and develop the kind of impervious mindset necessary to transcend their circumstances and create the lives they want. I founded the nonprofit *The Made 2 Change the World™ Foundation* to equip underserved youth with the tools, resources, and network they need to strengthen their mindset while empowering them with the knowledge, skills, and strategies necessary to become tomorrow's leaders. By so doing, they can affect global change and create a new future for themselves, their families, and their communities.

Of course, it's not just young people who need tools to create and maintain an impervious mindset. During the pandemic, many people were deeply shaken by fear, loss of employment, and lockdowns. In any such challenging times, it's imperative to find programs or connect with mentors that can help build or bolster your mindset so that you can stand strong, forge ahead, and overcome whatever obstacles appear.

3. The Power of Your Why

Fredrich Nietzsche once wrote, "The person who has a why to live for can bear almost any how." Your 'why' is your driving force, the fuel that energizes you, and the anchor that keeps you true to your mission and purpose. Your 'why' keeps you getting up and persevering no matter what. It won't let you take "no" for an answer, and it will drive you to find a way or make a way. When your 'why' is strong enough, you want to shout your message from the rooftops and share it with the world. You'll stand in your authenticity and power, and nothing will get between you and your success.

When clients come to me, before we work on anything else, I help them get clear on their 'why', their goals, and their message. Everyone has a story to tell, a message to share. In fact, someone in the world is waiting for you to share your message, as only you can! Together, we dig deep into why what you have to say is important, who it will impact, and what kind of difference you want to make for others. Once you understand and feel your personal, powerful, driving, emotional reasons for sharing your message with the world, you're ready to do the work that will amplify your impact.

What's *your* 'why'? What is the core reason you must succeed? And why must you do so *now*? A 2019 cancer diagnosis was the most recent moment that fueled my 'why'. As I sat in the doctor's office, I said to myself, "That's it—no more playing small. I am made to change the world. I am stepping out of the shadows, and into the full expression of myself. From this moment on, I will stand in my power, use my voice, and live every day as a force for good. I am here to help others do the same, so they can transform into the authentic, successful, and impactful individuals they were born to be."

The world needs your example and your message. I believe that you were made to change the world—but you need to be ready, willing, and committed enough to do the work. Remember that your voice matters, your message matters, and you matter. It's time for you to step into your power and your purpose. Write your new story. Develop an impervious mindset. And use the power of your 'why' as your fuel for success.

Master these three principles and the world will watch you soar!

About Ellie

"Ellie is a transformational leader who is changing the world!" ~ Jack Canfield

Ellie Shefi is the very definition of tenacious. Having overcome a lifetime of adversity, including abuse, domestic violence, homelessness, cancer, and a myriad of other health issues that have seen her defy the doctors' death deadlines for over two decades, Ellie has mastered mindset, resiliency, and resourcefulness, and she has dedicated her life to the empowerment of others.

Ellie is an attorney, entrepreneur, strategist, mentor, coach, teacher, trainer, philanthropist, and engaged community servant. She is a sought-after international speaker and award-winning author who is regularly featured in publications, and on podcasts, summits, and television shows.

A heart-centered, transformational leader who facilitates change, Ellie provides her clients with practical, easy-to-implement tools and strategies that generate results. Ellie helps entrepreneurs to bring their business to life; authors to get their book out of their head and into the world; speakers to amplify their message so they can scale their impact; and women to shed external labels and expectations, find their voice, stand in their power, and become the architects of their life and legacy.

Additionally, Ellie is the publisher of *Sisters Rising*™, a book series that provides women with a platform to tell their stories, showcase their businesses, and raise awareness of their work. She is also the founder of *The Made 2 Change the World*™ *Foundation*, a nonprofit that equips and empowers the next generation with the tools, resources, and strategies they need to create the lives, communities, and world they envision. To learn more about Ellie's work or how you can get involved with *The Made 2 Change the World*™ *Foundation*, please visit ellieshefi.com.

An award-winning author, Ellie's books include: *Unlocking Your Superpower: 8 Steps to Turn Your Existing Knowledge into Income; Sisters Rising: Stories of Remarkable Women Living Extraordinary Lives*; and *The Authorities: Powerful Wisdom from Leaders in the Field* (which she co-authored with multiple *New York Times* #1 bestselling authors Les Brown, Bob Proctor, Marci Shimoff, and Raymond Aaron). Ellie is also the co-author of the upcoming book, *Women Who Shine* (forthcoming Fall 2021).

Connect with Ellie at **ellieshefi.com** or **@ellieshefi** on:
- Facebook
- Instagram
- Twitter
- Clubhouse
- LinkedIn

CHAPTER 7

THE WITNESS

BY GEETHA KRISHNAMURTHI

It is a beautiful, clear, crisp fall Sunday at the end of September.

This day starts as the previous two days in a hotel in Indianapolis. A committed group of about 50-60 people gathered for an early morning yoga session. With many countries represented, one thing was clear. Everyone was drawn to this special being, this teacher, the one who bridges Science, Spirit, and Human Possibility with elegance. This teacher was the reason I was at the hotel.

None of us are immune to the inner pull or calling to move in a particular direction. Some of us flow towards it with a sense of wonder and curiosity. And some of us, the more resistant ones, come up with many reasons why it is the 'wrong' move to make.

I am the curious one, the one drawn by the inner voice, the voice I cannot ignore. This voice has led me to my many blessings in life.

This voice is the reason I became an energy medicine practitioner. This voice is the reason I did not *own* the stage II cancer diagnosis I was delivered a few years ago. This voice is the reason I was able to dissolve the impacted lymph nodes in my armpit within six months of diagnosis. This voice is the reason for the continued shrinking of my breast tumor. This voice is one I listen to and the one that guides me.

Several years earlier, this voice led me to this unique, charismatic teacher, Dr. Sue Morter, to continue my quest to understand, to learn, to delve into deep conversations of Quantum Science, energy, ancient wisdom, and healing. She brilliantly weaves all these aspects into lessons, and practical, day-to-day applications for the world we live and operate in. I learnt to embody and integrate these into my own life.

Never were these skills more needed than on this particular day for me.

Following the rich, guided meditation that afternoon, I took to the road, in my deep red Volvo, homeward bound to Toronto. The miles seem to glide past on the dry, open roads as the hands of the clock signal approach of the evening. I suddenly notice the huge, silvery, radiant full moon as it takes its seat to the horizon on my right, keeping company for the rest of the ride home. My heart is full. I am filled with gratitude for all the many blessings in my life, especially the magic of connection with a tribe of kindred souls.

A couple of hours west of my destination, I stop at an ONroute[1] station for gas and a break to stretch my legs. Quelling my disappointment at not being able to talk to my husband directly, I settle back into the seat for the remainder of the drive home.

Shortly after merging back on the busy stretch of this major highway, I noticed a slower-moving sedan in the middle lane ahead. I move to the lane on the left by the median separating oncoming traffic. As I got closer to passing the sedan to my right, out of the corner of my eye, I see the car veering into my lane.

---

1. ONroute is a Canadian service company which has the 50-year concession to operate highway rest areas.

Instinctively I act on the desire to avoid the inevitable, impending collision. Breaking at that close range, I knew, would be a sure way to prompt that which I was trying to avoid – colliding into the other car.

The limited options I had all pointed to some variation of a disastrous outcome. With no place to go, I swerved the steering wheel away from the intruding sedan. Of course, I did not account for Newton's first two laws of physics. My car violently snaked across the lane, hit the median several times, and spun across three live lanes of speeding traffic. I miss eighteen-wheelers plus other vehicles heading in my direction. I even miss a ten-foot ditch all the way to the right of the highway before flying over and landing into a field of the wild weed, goldenrod.

Miraculously, the car was still upright when I came to a standstill. Both airbags deployed, the air littered with acrid dust. The front windshield cracked like a flower. Stems of smoke spiraled through the hood. Yet, I was able to roll down my window in an effort to clear the air of smoke and airbag debris.

Time does slow down considerably, but only after the initial warp-speed events blur into immobility.

Suddenly, I spot a young man running down the slope towards my smoking car, urging me to get out of the car. "My mother is a nurse, and she's coming to help," he shouts. A few minutes later, the mother, Barb, appears as I stumble out of the car, shaking violently. She wraps her arms around me and whispers softly, "I got you honey, you're safe." I sag into Barb's enveloping arms. I draw on her strength as she slowly escorts me through the fields of goldenrod.

As we got close to the paved edge of the highway, a lady rushes out of another fully occupied vehicle towards us. Upon learning that I was the sole occupant of the car in the field, she quickly traces the sign of the cross on my forehead to bless me before rushing back to their vehicle. This family returning from a wedding in Michigan had stopped to call 911 to make sure that emergency personnel would be dispatched to tend to the mishap they saw unfold. Unsung heroes!

Barb still has a firm grip on me as we walk a few feet further along the edge of the highway to the family's waiting car. She guides me to sit on the passenger side in the front as she introduces me to her husband, Peter. Barb was the power I needed to pull and gather myself back together as we settle in to wait for the paramedics and police to arrive.

I learn as we wait that this kind family was on their way back from a family dinner in the area. Apparently, this family of three had front row seating to the series of events that led me to be sitting in their vehicle. In addition to coming to my aid physically, they generously offered to stay back to narrate what they watched unfold to the authorities.

As the paramedics brusquely cart me off to the waiting ambulance, citing privacy concerns, they refused to let Barb accompany me. And I miss the chance to get her contact details.

Once in the ambulance, the two young female paramedics immediately hook me up to various devices to get baseline vitals. Simultaneously, an Ontario Provincial Police Constable Ball comes in, curtly asks me a couple of questions, takes my driver's license, informs me that he'll meet me at the hospital, and promptly retreats. As the paramedics commence their tasks, I call on a friend and fellow energy medicine practitioner for relief. Through my labored breath, I give her a quick update, ask her to carry out remote healing treatment on me.

At the hospital, the triage nurse, along with other medical personnel, are quite surprised at the clarity and steadiness they see despite my difficulty breathing. I firmly decline their offer to take any pain medication. As painful as it was, I wanted to make sure I could gently guide my breath beyond the jugular notch at the top of my sternum all the way down to my belly. Knowing it was imperative to get my body into a repair and heal mode, I direct the breath away from the upper lobes of the lungs all the way down in and out of the belly.

Half a dozen x-rays later, when the doctor eventually comes in, clearly surprised with wide-eyes, he states that he sees no visible broken ribs or any organ impact. By the third-round of checks on my vitals, my blood pressure is back in the normal range. This, in spite of not being able to breathe fluidly more than an inch deep into my chest.

The police officer who finally tracks me to the hospital is a very different man. This Constable turns out to be kind, caring, and cheery. He even shared a memorable-stop-on-the-highway story about the weed, goldenrod. The officer who met me at the hospital confirmed that all I had been drinking was just plain water laced with lemon slices. Constable Ball discloses that Barb, Peter, and their son stayed at the scene to give him a full account of what they had witnessed. He confirms that because of this family's decision to act and, most importantly, give their eye-witness account of the events, I would not be charged with reckless driving.

Even though I had already thanked Barb while in their car, I wasn't sure I had expressed my heartfelt appreciation for what they did for me. When I ruefully commented at not having thanked this special family properly, the officer assured me that he had on my behalf.

At my husband's insistence, a couple of days later we went to see our family doctor, 'Dr. D' as he is affectionately known. Dr. D, a sweet, gentle man in his mid-seventies, was in utter disbelief that I was still upright and breathing. After a thorough physical examination, including many range-of-movement assessments, he shared that he had only seen two types of people survive such intense accidents - those who were unconscious and those with high blood-alcohol levels. Dr. D admitted that in all his years of practice, he had *never* seen anyone, completely conscious, undergo such an intense, physical experience with not a single broken bone or whiplash. He could not absorb that *'just'* doing three days of yoga, meditation, specific breathwork, etc., was the reason I was so pliable that I had, in essence, *escaped completely unscathed* from this ordeal.

Ultimately, this is a just tale of *gratitude.*

And, there are three potent reminders:

Number 1: Be a sponge – keep learning so applying becomes second-nature

Do not underestimate the role of a teacher or mentor in life. Take advantage of access to your mentors in life. Whether the skill is one where I learnt what it takes to pick up the phone for a cold-call, technique related or how to breathe, my teachers have all been instrumental in my evolution.

For months and years prior to this event, I was immersed in teachings of yoga, meditation, and breathwork. It was the influence of these teachings that led me to constantly be engaged in applying these teachings in the in-between moments of life. This was the only reason I was able to drop into my breath in a flash when it mattered most. My mind and consequently my body stayed out of flight-fight-freeze reflex typical of such extreme experiences. I had established strong neural pathways to my other two brains, gut and heart, allowing the body to be extremely pliable in the face of this intense episode.

Number 2: Be always in Gratitude

The power of gratitude is immense. Look around. There are countless things in our lives that we can take delight in being grateful for in the moment. Every single thing happens "for us," even though at the moment it may be hard to fathom.

Looking back, when the car started to spin, I instinctively leaned into the teachings. I am still in awe and gratitude for this intense event without which I may have never known I was capable of trading the normal knee-jerk reactions to a life-affirming one. I would still be oblivious to the gifts of potentiality within, and for that, I am extremely grateful to the person who initiated this chain of events.

Number 3: Be kind and caring

Yes, to be kind and caring is a choice we make every single moment. It may not be fashionable, but there is nothing quite like it to impact and influence someone's life. While we are often bombarded by the loud and coarse few who demand attention, it is easy to miss the softness of the kind ones around us.

Every single person who came to my aid and support, whether by deed or word, no matter how fleeting our encounter, was an earth-angel. All those who rush to assist someone in need, call 911, stop to help someone in trouble, offer a hand, a kind word, or gentle smile. There are many generous, kind, caring earth-angels that walk amongst us. You, too, are an earth-angel for someone on your path.

In the moment I felt the car slide and slowly spin, I focused my attention inward.

> I was *totally* in my body.
> I was *completely* awake and conscious.
> I was *in* my breath.
> I was *the* breath.
> *I was the Observer, the Witness within.*

> *...And in the moment, I was Awareness itself.*

About Geetha

Geetha Krishnamurthi has had a life-long interest in holistic approaches to health but, as a former corporate executive and entrepreneur, her advent into Energy Medicine came through an unlikely source.

In 2011, Nerian, her German Shepherd puppy, was struck with an illness that left him in severe pain and unable to stand. Overnight, simple tasks like eating and hygiene became an ordeal for the puppy. Weeks of medical appointments and strong medications that taxed Nerian's still-young body offered no relief.

Desperate for help, Geetha took Nerian to the world-renowned veterinary practice at the University of Guelph, Ontario, where doctors identified a rare bacterial infection. Relieved to finally have a diagnosis, it still took months of physiotherapy before Nerian could walk well again.

Geetha, determined to find a way to help Nerian avoid another such ordeal in future, attended a seminar to learn about clearing interferences in the energy field. Geetha knew instantly that she'd found the perfect modality to help her pup. This led her to learn Bio-Energetic Synchronization Technique (B.E.S.T.) founded by Dr. M. T. Morter Jr.

Her journey to learn about the body's amazing capacity to heal led her to study for the B.E.S.T. Animal Mastery certification before even realizing that she could also help people with this technique! Driven by her mission to support others, Geetha continued her journey by studying with some of Energy Medicine's top practitioners, including Dr. Roland Francis Phillips and Dr. Sue Morter, author of *The Energy Codes*, and daughter of B.E.S.T. founder Dr. M. T. Morter Jr.

Time and again, Geetha was able to help clients where traditional medicine had fallen short. Along the way, however, something remarkable happened: Geetha experienced her own healing transformation that allowed her to finally release the trauma from years of unsuccessful fertility treatments.

Today, Geetha heads' *Insightful Perspectives Group*, a private membership association, dedicated to helping people and animals clear the subconscious interferences that keep them from achieving their maximum potential. This may translate, in health, as a physical, mental and/or emotional aspect; in life, as inner-peace, release from the grip of 'stress', goals that flow with ease, etc. As an effective results-orientated trainer, coach, and energy medicine practitioner, Geetha has travelled the globe to both teach and train others.

Geetha believes that every person can and should experience abundance in all areas of their life. Driven by curiosity to learn, a desire to always improve, and dedication to healing, Geetha puts this belief into her ongoing work with clients, whether as a teacher, coach, or energy medicine practitioner.

Geetha currently lives in Toronto with her family. She offers healing sessions with clients in-person, at her office as well as remotely, teaches students across the globe, and leads online and in-person classes and seminars.

Her repertoire of credentials includes:
- Certified Human Behavior Consultant (DISC);
- Certified Professional Coach;
- Certified T.E.P. Practitioner;
- Animal Master B.E.S.T. Practitioner;
- Elite Master B.E.S.T. Practitioner;
- Spiritual B.E.S.T. Practitioner;
- Certified Energy Codes® Facilitator;
- Certified Energy Codes® Practitioner;
- Certified Energy Codes® Master Trainer;
- Certified Energy Codes® Coach.

You can connect with Geetha at:
- Geetha.Krishnamurthi@gmail.com
- (866) 588-4615
- www.facebook.com/geetha.krishnamurthi.9

CHAPTER 8

YOUR DIGITAL DNA: THE BUILDING BLOCKS OF YOUR ONLINE SUCCESS

BY NICK NANTON & JW DICKS

The universe is made of stories, not atoms.
~ Muriel Rukeyser

Back in the Stone Age—aka, before the internet—your professional reputation was squarely in the hands of the people you associated with. As long as you were honest, reliable and straightforward in your business dealings, that reputation stayed spotless. And whatever you did behind closed doors rarely, if ever, spilled out into your professional world.

Fast forward to today, where, thanks to posts on social media sites and elsewhere on the internet, you're suddenly stuck explaining things you don't want to have to explain to the people you do business with. Those things may seem relatively harmless, but those pictures of you on vacation after a few drinks will suddenly become part of the professional conversation about you.

Your reputation is now at the mercy of Google, Bing and other internet search engines. Think about it: The first thing most of us do when we hear about someone we're interested in doing business with is to do a search on their name to see what we can find out. What we find out on that first page of results is critical to how we will view them professionally.

That's why we've spent a lot of time—and an awful lot of money—to unlock the secrets behind all of our "Digital DNA." What we found out can boost your profile, lift your business to the next level, and make you an online superstar.
How? Read on.

BUILDING CELEBRITY EXPERTS

Our agency specializes in building Celebrity Expert® status for our clients. While they're experts in their field, they don't know how to position themselves in their market with the right media for their particular message.

Just like a great movie or book needs the proper publicity launch to make the public aware of their existence, our clients need a certain kind of exposure to communicate their unique personalities, skill sets and experiences to a broader circle of other influential thought leaders and potential customers. We work at making the right connections for them at the right time, using such platforms as bestselling books, programs on network TV affiliates, and articles in national periodicals such as *The Wall Street Journal, Newsweek* and *USA Today.*

Naturally, we promote these media placements through our clients' websites and social media services, such as Facebook, Twitter and so forth, to further boost their brands. This ensures that these prestigious appearances show up as an integral part of their online identity. Note, however, that we said *"part"* of that identity.

The fact is there are a lot of facets to anyone's online identity that we don't control in this process. There may still be a lot of other personal or even professional information that might show up that could easily conflict with the main messaging we are putting out about them.

For all the information about yourself that either you or other people leave behind online, we've developed the term Digital DNA™. Unlike genetic DNA, this "strand" is one you actually can alter to your benefit. And it can definitely be in your best interests to do so.

GOING DEEPER INTO YOUR DIGITAL DNA™

As we said, your Digital DNA™ is comprised of every byte of information that exists about you in the online world. We're talking about your personal websites and blog posts, Facebook, LinkedIn, YouTube, personal photos, press about you and any other internet site where you've been mentioned or where you've posted something.

If you're like most people, you've probably Googled your name at some point and either been either surprised at the information that's appeared about you—or disappointed that you haven't left more of an online mark. The good news is that both situations can be corrected and should be. Understanding and controlling how you're represented on the internet is the single most important business strategy you should undertake today because again, that's where everyone at this moment in time goes to find out who you are, what you do, and whether you're the person they want to do business with. It's almost like the ultimate job interview—and one that you're not even in the room for!

It's easy to see that your Digital DNA™ contains the building blocks of your success, but it only works that way if it is properly managed and continually updated. If it isn't, your online reputation will remain a big question mark, controlled by unknown factors or even worse, actually tarnished by other parties you may not even know.

Your offline activities now pale beside your online reputation, which is more easily accessible than ever, because most of us have the internet at our fingertips 24/7. When people want to know about you, they'll instantly jump on their laptop, iPad or smartphone and find out what they can. Even if someone offline personally vouches for you, the internet has become our de facto authority and can trump that recommendation.

That's because, while our memories can fade and grow fuzzy, online info remains as clear as it was the day it was posted, which might have been two, 10 or even 15 years ago. Whatever was said about you in the past, good or bad, right or wrong, isn't going away any day soon.

Because information about you told by anyone right or wrong is so readily available to anyone checking you out, you must be constantly aware of your Digital DNA™—and be proactive in controlling what story is being projected online to prospects and customers. This is a quantum shift in how people find out about you and check you out, and many people still haven't caught on to its importance. To ignore the reality of this shift and its consequences, however, is to unnecessarily put your business and reputation at risk.

OUTCLASSING THE COMPETITION

Even if you're confident there's nothing out there online that can really hurt you, there's also an awesome opportunity to use your Digital DNA™, if you're willing to be proactive about it. Controlling your online reputation in order to present yourself in the best possible light to all who search for you means you'll be taking advantage of the incredible untapped potential that the internet offers you to boost your expert status.

As we said, when people perform an online search on your name, it's like the ultimate job interview. Now, imagine going to a job interview in a t-shirt and shorts, instead of your best clothes, that would be more than a little bit crazy, right? Well, not attending to your Digital DNA™ isn't that far from that outlandish example. In every other business situation, you want to look your best, and this vital one is no different?

Odds are your competition is already hard at work making sure they look *their* best online. Just as you wouldn't be the only applicant participating in a job interview process, you most certainly have other people selling what you're selling online. Your goal should be to "look" better than they do, so you have the leadership position in your field all to yourself. Whoever takes that position as the primary online expert has an obvious and undeniable advantage—and forces everyone else to play catch-up.

When you work your Digital DNA™ to the max, you put yourself in that leadership position.

CLEANING UP YOUR DIGITAL DNA™

The first move you should make to really take control of your DNA is to clean up and cement your current online identity as much as you can. There are four important steps you can take to make that happen.

1. Manage Your Brand

As you set out to tweak your online presence, first *write out who you want to be seen* as when people Google you. Keep that paper with you—and keep that personal image in mind as you participate in online activities of all kinds. Build toward that digital brand. Think of it as a goal and take small steps every day to make it a reality. A great idea is to set aside a half-hour to an hour a day just to focus on your online identity. This can be done by writing blogs and doing a press release on the blog you wrote. When you syndicate the press release it will be picked up by online media services, and many will then be posted by the search engines and either the press release, blog or both will appear in a Google search about you. If you do this daily, you'll be adding 365 more items to your Digital DNA™, which will help drive conflicting information about you lower on the search page.

2. Create Consistency

You must make your personal page on Facebook (if you have one) as professional as possible, and make sure all your social media pages reflect the same "you." It's great to showcase family, pets and all other personal activities that show you in a positive light—you just have to make sure nothing shows up that would *conflict with or contradict the online image you want to put out there.* When you post a picture online with you in it, ask yourself whether you want a future employer to see this picture because there's a good chance they will.

3. Own Your name

You might be thinking it's more trouble than it's worth to participate in Twitter, Facebook and the like. The advantage, though, of doing that is that the more places you put your name, the more SEO power your Digital DNA™ acquires. Sometimes just a couple of "tweets" can put your name on the first page of Google results—just remember to write about things you want to be associated with!

4. Be Yourself

This might seem to contradict everything we've just discussed, but as the old marketing motto goes, "People buy people." Working with your personality, instead of against it, brings more authentic results than trying to be something you're not. Obviously, you want to put some filters in place and not recount some horrific fight you might have had with your spouse the other night, but you can still use appropriate humor as well as share your hobbies so people can see you're a well-rounded and interesting person.

The key to all of this is follow-through. When you stay on this effort day-in and day-out, it continues to pay off and keeps your name at the top of the online heap.

GOING TO THE NEXT LEVEL

Yes, there's a lot you can do on your own to fine-tune your Digital DNA™ but, at some point, if you're going to want to really make your online reputation pop out in a meaningful and awesome way, getting some expert help is really the best solution.

That's because, to really get proactive with your Digital DNA™ takes a lot of effort and time, as well as some specific skill sets that you may not have. For example, you'll want to distribute online press releases and syndicate them to high-impact sites to really trumpet your business accomplishments and media appearances. You'll also want to consider posting videos based around your area of expertise, as well as creating original content in the form of articles, blogs, webinars, and e-books. This kind of content is important to have posted at different places other than your own personal website. That way, when your name is Googled, you'll look incredibly influential all across the internet.

And speaking of your own website, you'll also want to make sure your website avails itself of the latest SEO techniques, so that it (and you) ranks as high as possible in search engine results.

Putting all these kinds of things in motion really helps you sparkle online. When you create and continue to update a comprehensive and compelling social media presence, as well as generate the content we just described, the more positive "buzz" builds around your name. You decrease the digital "noise" while turning up the volume (and increasing the focus) on your credentials and accomplishments.

That's important, because the more positive content that's connected to you, the higher you rank in online search engines.

That directly affects your bottom line in a way you often don't even see, because it's hard to know how much business you're losing, simply because your online "story" isn't coming across correctly. All you can know is that the result is a negative ROI.

There's one thing that science has proved over the years: small changes can have profound effects. Every step you take to promote yourself online in an authentic and impactful way will increase the chance that a prospect will quickly understand the unique features and benefits you alone can provide. At the same time, each informative link you provide back to your talents and services is a new pathway to greater respect and increased revenue.

Whether you know it or not, your Digital DNA™ is already out there—and is directly responsible for whether a potential customer will buy from you or not. If you don't take control of it, it can't work to its fullest extent for you. Even worse, it might even be working against you. By taking action, you have the ability to create an overwhelmingly positive perception that positions you as the celebrity expert in your field. That ultimately results in more sales and increased profits—and isn't that really the best inheritance you can get from your DNA?

About Nick

An Emmy Award-Winning Director and Producer, Nick Nanton, Esq., produces media and branded content for top thought leaders and media personalities around the world.

Recognized as a leading expert on branding and storytelling, Nick has authored more than two dozen Best-Selling books (including *The Wall Street Journal* Best-Seller, *StorySelling*™) and produced and directed more than 65 documentaries, earning 22 Emmy Awards and 43 nominations. Nick speaks to audiences internationally on the topics of branding, entertainment, media, business and storytelling at major universities and events.

As the CEO of DNA Media, Nick oversees a portfolio of companies including: The Dicks + Nanton Agency (an international agency with more than 3,000 clients in 63 countries), Dicks + Nanton Productions, Ambitious.com and DNA Films. Nick is an award-winning director, producer and songwriter who has worked on everything from large scale events to documentaries with the likes of Tony Robbins, Ivanka Trump, Sir Richard Branson, Larry King, Jack Nicklaus, Rudy Ruettiger (inspiration for the Hollywood Blockbuster, *RUDY*), Dick Vitale, Brian Tracy, Jack Canfield (*The Secret*, creator of the *Chicken Soup for the Soul*® Series), and many more.

Nick has been seen in *USA Today, The Wall Street Journal, Newsweek, BusinessWeek, Inc. Magazine, The New York Times, Entrepreneur*® *Magazine, Forbes* and *Fast Company*, and has appeared on ABC, NBC, CBS, and FOX television affiliates across the country, as well as on The Biography Channel, CNN, FOX News, CNBC, and MSNBC coast-to-coast.

Nick is a member of the Florida Bar, a member of The National Academy of Television Arts & Sciences (Home to the Emmys), and co-founder of The National Academy of Best-Selling Authors®. He was a recipient of the Global Shield Humanitarian Award in Feb. 2019.

Nick also enjoys serving as an Elder at Orangewood Church, supporting Young Life, and rooting for the Florida Gators with his wife Kristina and their three children, Brock, Bowen and Addison…and their two dogs Ella and Emmitt.

Learn more at:
- www.NickNanton.com
- www.DNAmedia.com

About JW

JW Dicks, Esq., is the CEO of DN Agency, an Inc. 5000 Multimedia Company that represents over 3,000 clients in 63 countries.

He is a *Wall Street Journal* Best-Selling Author® who has authored or co-authored over 47 books, a 7-time Emmy® Award-winning Executive Producer and a Broadway Show Producer.

JW is Chairman of the Board of the National Academy of Best-Selling Authors®, Board Member of the National Association of Experts, Writers and Speakers®, and a Board Member of the International Academy of Film Makers®.

He has been quoted on business and financial topics in national media such as *USA Today, The Wall Street Journal, Newsweek, Forbes, CNBC.com*, and *Fortune Magazine Small Business*.

JW has co-authored books with legends like Jack Canfield, Brian Tracy, Tom Hopkins, Dr. Nido Qubein, Steve Forbes, Richard Branson, Michael Gerber, Dr. Ivan Misner, and Dan Kennedy.

JW has appeared and interviewed on business television shows airing on ABC, NBC, CBS, and FOX affiliates around the country.

JW and his wife of 49 years, Linda, have two daughters, and four granddaughters. He is a sixth-generation Floridian and splits his time between his home in Orlando and his beach house on Florida's west coast.

CHAPTER 9

MENTAL-SWITCH
HOW I OVERCAME MY DEPRESSION AND CREATED MASSIVE SUCCESS IN BUSINESS AND LIFE

BY NIDHIKA BAHL

It was the year 2008. In the eyes of the world, I was super successful. I had been educated at the best institutes recognized globally. I had been working with the best corporate houses across the globe. I made a lot of money, much more than my peers. I also had a seemingly good marriage. I lived in a beautiful home, drove fancy cars, ate at expensive restaurants, and used only luxury brands.

The reality, however, was completely different. I was this superwoman on the surface, but underneath, I was a little lost girl who needed help desperately. Within the last nine months, I had lost my father, marriage, career, health, a sense of purpose, and self-esteem. Grieving and in denial, I had become a loner, a prisoner in my own home. I avoided all social contact and could not do the simplest of tasks. For months I believed there was nothing I could do about the way I felt.

I was so afraid of the shame and judgment of anyone finding

out about my inner pain and sadness. I cried! I cried over the unfairness of it all. I cried because I longed for the happiness that I perceived in the lives of others. All I ever dreamt of was a beautiful home and a loving family. And look where I had landed myself. My internal voice constantly told me how hopeless and pathetic my life was. I just wanted to kill myself. My life was an enormous mess, and I did not know how to make it right. I felt powerless!

I am sure you are wondering what changed. How did I go from being clinically depressed in 2008 to penning this book in 2021?

MENTAL-SWITCH!

In the fourth year of my fight against depression, I was introduced to self-help books. Truth be told, I had never been a reader. All I ever read were textbooks from school. I did understand novels, but self-help books – what are they? I had no clue! Reluctantly, I started reading the first book. To my surprise, I loved it so much that I got hooked on to reading. That year I read near 300 books, almost a book a day.

Finally, I found a book called *Battlefield of the Mind* by Joyce Meyer. The book's message urged me to look up Joyce on Google and, I came across a YouTube recording of her women's conference. I started watching the video hoping to get answers to the questions in my mind. Somewhere around the 40-minute mark, one lady in the audience raised her hand to ask a question. To my surprise, she asked Joyce the exact "Why Me" question that had been playing in my mind for over three years. I jumped on my seat eagerly, waiting to hear Joyce's response, and then Joyce said something that changed the entire course of my life!

She said to the lady, "You hurt; you heal, you help."

She explained to that lady that you are the chosen one. God has a plan for your life. He has faith in your ability to bounce back from this adversity, and when you do, you can be his channel to help others do the same.

Those words from Joyce changed the whole trajectory of my life. Rather than viewing myself as a victim, I started seeing myself as a hero, a protagonist! I knew there was a huge calling in my life. I was going to help others with my experience. And at that moment, I resolved to turn my life around.

It still took another year from that time to finally receive the pink slip from my therapist and be told – you are good to go! And it was not like life was a bed of roses post that. I had to start from scratch in every area of my life. Every day I had to choose whether to quit or keep moving. That was hard. But I am glad I made the "right" choice each time.

And today, when I look back, I genuinely believe that depression was the best thing that ever happened to me. It made me fearless. I would never have been who I am today without having gone through that experience.

If you were to take just one thing from what I have shared about my comeback journey, it's this:

"YOUR PAST IS NOT YOUR FUTURE"

I don't know what's your dream. I don't even know what situation you are facing. I don't know how hard things are for you. All I know is that you can turn your life around if you keep making the right choices. There will be good days, there will be bad days, and you know what, there will be good days again! Just know that if there's no enemy within, the enemy outside can do you no harm. *The battlefield is in your mind.* You're the only one who can change things for yourself. Please don't run from your pain. Embrace it and allow it to become your driving force. If you want this decade of your life to be the best, say "Yes" to your dreams, say "Yes" to your potential and say "Yes" to the 'extraordinary' within you waiting to be unleashed!

Ready to get to work? Let's go!

11 ESSENTIAL STEPS TO SUCCESS

Even though it is tempting to believe that your good intentions could outwork the necessary action to achieve your dreams, the reality is quite the opposite. For any transformation to occur, you should have a positive bias towards action in the right direction. There are *'11 Essential Steps'* you must take to realize your dreams. Consider these as your guideposts on the road to success — directing you to keep moving towards the life you truly desire.

Step 1: Take Responsibility

Embrace reality and take responsibility for where you are in life. Don't make excuses or blame others. Just focus on what you can do. The deciding factor in success is never the external factors; it is how you choose to respond to them. Don't insist on how things "should" be. Things that seem "bad" at a personal level always look different from a higher perspective.

Pain + Reflection = Progress.

Do reflect calmly during/after a painful experience to breakthrough to a higher level. Accept where you are and determine where you are going to be.

Step 2: Set Clear Audacious Goals

Set audacious goals that will push you to live life from your highest potential. Choose your priorities (based on your values) and reject the rest. Don't confuse trappings of success (e.g., job title, money, and status) with what gives you real, long-term happiness. The world is full of opinions. Don't let them influence where you want to be in life. Follow your heart and walk that path, regardless of other people's views. You will never be happy in life unless you live the life you want to live. Don't wear masks just to fit into this world, be true to yourself and walk in the direction you want.

Step 3: Quit The Need For Perfection

Sloppy success is better than perfect mediocrity. Many self-help books focus on starting strong. While it is a good idea to have a plan, it is a bad idea to strive for a perfect plan. Know that the starting plan is merely your jump-off point. There's no such thing as a perfect plan; the plan you start with will not be the same plan that brings you success. However, it would help if you started with your first plan to take your initial steps, start the learning journey and refine your course.

Step 4: Take Action Daily

Consistently repeated daily actions + time = unconquerable results.

If you improve by 1% every day, you don't just become 365% or 3.7 times better in 1 year. Thanks to the compounding effect, you become 37 times better. The reverse is also true. Thus, irrespective of where you are now, your actions define your trajectory and future outcomes (for better or worse). Taking daily action is essential to creating desired success. You can use time-blocking to prevent your time from being hijacked by unplanned activities and protect your "performance time" for your most strategic/vital actions.

Step 5: Make A Commitment

Greatness doesn't come when significant results are achieved; it comes from an accumulation of countless decisions and moments when someone does what's needed, even when he/she doesn't feel like it. Commitment is about doing whatever it takes to keep the promises you've made to yourself and others. Keeping your promises with others creates trust and builds strong relationships. Keeping your promises with yourself builds your self-esteem and character.

Also, committing to your goals 100% is way easier than committing 99%. When you pursue your goals with 99% commitment, you're leaving a little bit of doubt in your mind, which causes you to lose precious willpower throughout the day. For example, if you commit to exercising only 99% of the time every day, you are going to have a mental battle about whether or not you want to exercise, and sooner or later, you are going to falter. But if you come in with 100% commitment, it will be a lot easier for you because now you haven't left yourself a choice. It is raining outside, and you can't go for a run. Well, too bad, you are going to do an in-home workout!

Step 6: Measure Your Progress

You won't know how well or badly you are doing unless you keep score. Use measurements as a feedback tool to identify where you stand and what you must do to improve and achieve your goals. Define and measure the lead indicators and lag indicators for every goal. Lag indicators are the results you want to achieve (e.g., lose X pounds). Lead indicators are the activities that deliver those results (e.g., number of weekly cardio exercises). You have more control over the lead indicators than lag indicators. By measuring both, you're tracking both your strategy and execution. If you miss your goals, you can diagnose if it's due to the wrong strategy or a failure to execute it.

Step 7: Don't Let Mistakes Become Failures

Our ego leads us to reject our mistakes and weaknesses. When others point out our blind spots, we tend to react defensively. When our emotions hijack our logic, we act irrationally. To achieve success in life, you must be radically open-minded, give up your need to be right, and always use data to course-correct as you go along.

Step 8: Harness The Power Of Momentum

When you try to accomplish something new in life, you are cutting through the winds of resistance, and the momentum is not on your side. This lack of speed might cause you to look worse than you are. It may create extreme self-doubt – you may feel that you don't quite have it in you to make it to your goals. You may even quit on your dreams as a result. But before you do that, remember that the only way to make momentum work for you is to create it. And to do that, you have to stay engaged in the process even when you feel like quitting.

Step 9: Invest In Yourself

Learning is a lifelong process. Engaging in continuous learning will open your mind to possibilities. You could read books, listen to educational audios, attend workshops and seminars or even join a mastermind group. Being part of a community of like-minded people where growth is modeled and expected will keep you on the path to success.

Step 10: Quit Trying To Create Work-Life Balance

One of the most frequent laments I hear as a coach is, "I need more balance," a common mantra for what's missing in most lives. We hear about work-life balance so much; we automatically assume that's what we should be seeking. It's not. Extraordinary results demand focused action. When you focus on your priorities and act on your goals, you'll automatically go out of balance. The challenge then is not preventing going out of balance, for you must. The challenge becomes how long you stay on priority and out of balance. Leaving some things unfinished is a necessary trade-off for extraordinary results. But you can't leave everything unfinished, and that's where counterbalancing comes in.

You must never go so much out of balance that you can't find your way back or stay so long away from your life and family that nothing or nobody is waiting for you when you return. Here are my two cents on this. Don't try to balance. Prioritize. When you're supposed to be working, work, and when you're supposed to be enjoying, enjoy. Be fully present at the moment.

Step 11: Be In A State Of P. E. A. C. E.

Peace is the absence of mental stress or anxiety, a state of calmness that comes when everything coexists in perfect harmony. Follow these success rituals to keep yourself in a peaceful state while pursuing your goals.

- *Practice Mindfulness*
  By slowing down and getting aware of what is in and around us, we can bring peace and joy to ourselves and others. You could do this by coloring a mandala, reading scripture, listening to healing music, or simply sitting in stillness.

- *Express Your Emotions*
  Most of us keep our negative emotions locked inside us and tell ourselves, "I shouldn't feel this way!" We judge our emotions and stop ourselves from experiencing them. These bottled-up emotions eventually show up in our bodies as psychosomatic diseases. Venting your feelings in an imaginary letter can help you maintain emotional balance. The more you do it, the easier life will be for you. You will get rid of all the clutter in your head, and you will be able to think clearly about your life.

- *Appreciate Yourself And Others*
  Gratitude is vital to joy, and joy is crucial to success. You can set the tone for the whole day by intentionally giving just five minutes of your time to acknowledge and appreciate all the good things in your life.

- **_Celebrate Small Wins Daily_**
  Be highly intentional and deliberate about 'celebrating all your wins' and rewarding yourself for them daily. And each time you do that, you will send a positive reinforcement to your brain, motivating it to recreate the desired winning behavior.

- **_Engage In Joyful "Me-Time" Activities_**
  Take care of yourself by making time for doing things _you_ love to do. Frustrating and neglecting yourself in the pursuit of making everyone else happy is neither going to serve you nor them in the long run. There is a difference in being there for others, from a position of duty versus a position of love and genuine care.

About Nidhika

Nidhika Bahl is an International Bestselling Author, India's Leading Life and Success Coach, Holistic Healer, Strategic Interventionist, and Mental-Switch Specialist.

She works as a leading expert in creating peak performance for celebrities, athletes, entrepreneurs, high-performing business leaders, corporate professionals, and educators. *(Her client Manushi Chhillar was crowned Miss World in 2017.)*

Throughout her career, Nidhika has mentored tens of thousands of entrepreneurs and other global achievers through private programs, mastermind groups, and one-on-one coaching. She has continued to refine and integrate over two decades of high-achievement distinctions, principles, and insights into a well-structured learning system called *The Game Of Life®*. Her highly valued, actionable, and results-oriented content, along with her witty and engaging style, has made her a favored keynote to audiences, large and small, across the globe.

Nidhika is also the Talk Show Host of two popular web series - *India's Biggest Comebacks* and *Invincibles With Nidhika Bahl*. She also hosts a podcast series called the *Mental-Switch* on Spotify, Google Podcasts, and Apple Podcasts.

Nidhika is regularly featured/quoted in multiple national and international newspapers and magazines like *Forbes, Economic Times, Bombay Times, Femina, Vogue, Cosmopolitan, Mid-Day, Mumbai Mirror, Pune Mirror, Bangalore Mirror, Tata Sky,* International FM Channels, NBC, ABC, CBS News, and FOX.

During her growth journey, Nidhika was trained and mentored by some of the great teacher leaders of the 21st century – Anthony Robbins, T. Harv Eker, Blair Singer, Robert Kiyosaki, Les Brown, Alex Mandossian, Paul Martinelli, Dr. Randin Brons, Denis Waitley, Clinton Swaine, Larry Gilman, Roddy Galbraith, Brian Tracy, Gerry Robert, and John C. Maxwell.

By Qualification, Nidhika is a Certified Coach, Teacher and Speaker with The John Maxwell Team, an Internationally Certified Success Coach, Master

SPIRIT Life Coach, Theta Healing® Practitioner, Access Bars® Facilitator, Clearing Practitioner, Lama Fera Practitioner, BACH Flower Remedies Practitioner, Akashic Records Advanced Practitioner, Internationally Certified Master Facilitator, NLP (Neuro-linguistic Programming) Master Practitioner, Certified Ho'oponopono Practitioner, Creator of 'The White Rainbow Access' to Extrasensory Perception and Life Transformation Coach.

Nidhika has won numerous awards for excellence in Training, Coaching, and Consulting, including – The 'Distinguished Trainer' award by the Times Ascent World HRD Congress at the National Awards For Excellence In Training & Development and also at the Asia Training & Development Awards, Singapore, 'Award For Best-In-Class Life Coach & Facilitator' at the Asia Coaching Leadership Excellence Awards, Singapore, Award of 'Exceptional Women Of Excellence' at the Women Economic Forum, 'Top 100 Global Coaching Leaders' award at the 26th Edition of the Times Ascent World HRD Congress, Femina 'Women Icon Of The Year' Award at the 5th World Women Leadership Congress and most recently 'Celebrity Life Coach Of The Year' award at the International Quality Awards.

Nidhika is obsessed with providing solutions that inspire people to move out of mediocrity and take a front-row seat in their lives, living life out of their highest potential.

You can connect with Nidhika at:

- Email: nidhika@nidhikabahl.com
- Web: www.nidhikabahl.com
- Facebook: www.facebook.com/author.nidhikabahl
- Instagram: @nidhikabahl

CHAPTER 10

I GET KNOCKED DOWN, *BUT* I GET UP AGAIN

BY ILYA VITA

The greatest glory in living lies not in never falling,
but in rising every time we fall.
~ Nelson Mandela

There are so many times we get knocked down in life—the loss of a job, the death of a loved one, an illness, a divorce, betrayal, etc. For myself, I have been knocked down so many times that I sometimes wonder if I have spent more time down, getting up, or actually being up.

The most important thing is that you rise up higher than you were when you got knocked down. When we rise, we learn, grow, and become who we need to be to achieve greatness. To better understand, I will share my last knockdown, which occurred in two separate phases in my life. To understand these phases, you'll need a little history.

I grew up in a small town with older non-biological parents. My mother had a brain tumor when I was seven. It was removed, but then she suffered an aneurism while in the hospital. Due to this, some brain matter was severely damaged. What was returned home was no longer my mother. She was in a wheelchair, diabetic, morbidly obese, hypertensive, delusional, and meaner than a rattlesnake. Just like a rattlesnake, you didn't know when she would strike. She had guns and large knives at her disposal. If she was not verbally or physically attacking my father, it was aimed at me. I lived in a war zone, never sure if I was going to make it out alive.

In addition to the chaos, she was in and out of the hospital with physical and mental impairments. Soon after, my grandmother moved in with dementia, had a stroke, and a heart attack. Then my father became ill, and he had several strokes, too many to count. Later, my father had a heart attack and open-heart surgery. At ten years of age, I became the parent to my grandmother, mother, and father. This included wound care, medication management, injections of insulin, doctors' appointments, cooking, cleaning, and so much more.

Flash forward a few years....

I moved out of the home the day after my 17th birthday, with a man that I had only spoken to on the phone and exchanged a picture with. He was 12 years older than me. You can do the math. Does this give you an indication of the level of my desperation?

When I moved out, I took more than my suitcase. I also took with me PTSD, depression, an inability to feel and show emotions, and I am sure much more. I had many years of mental health counseling and medications once I left, but the demons of my past continued to plague me.

In the first phase, toward the end of 2007, I hit rock bottom. I had moved from Las Vegas to Washington State, fleeing from a business partner who became a stalker. This was someone who threatened to harm my children. I lost my business, income, home, dogs, sent my son to live with his father, and my identity of who I thought I was. Looking back, I can see the PTSD and anxiety were growing stronger and stronger.

Washington State, especially the area that I was living in, is not known for its sunshine, so that contributed to my depression. I had night terrors and then developed disassociation with amnesia. My mental health was a hot mess, to say the least. I was not only on the crazy train, but I was also the conductor.

My mental health train finally derailed toward the end of 2008. I had two suicide attempts. The last attempt bought me a ticket into a required stay at a psychiatric hospital. That was the first time I was told that I had a serious mental illness. It was also suggested that I look into Social Security Disability.

Upon release, I saw more therapists, each confirming that I had Bi-polar, Manic Depressive, Suicidal Ideation, and a few other conditions sprinkled in here and there. Before the "breakdown," I used to love to drive. I had been so independent, confident in my abilities, and accomplished. After the breakdown, I could no longer go out into the public on my own. Cooking, something that I enjoyed and excelled at, was too many steps. Showering was a two-hour process.

I applied for Social Security benefits and, as per the protocol, was denied. No one wanted to hire someone that had to bring a support human wherever they went. Or someone who went from hyper to sleeping all day and could not complete even the simplest of tasks. So, I reapplied with the help of an attorney. I went before a psychiatrist of Social Security's choosing and was found disabled. This did not mean that I did not want to get better; I wanted that more than air. I knew the woman I used to be and wanted to not only find her but find a better version.

Then my miracle came, a therapist named Marcia. Marcia was amazing, kind, and caring. She introduced me to Dialectical Behavior Therapy (DBT). With Marcia's help, I started making some slow improvements. By this time, I was living in a VERY small town. I could drive the three or four blocks to the store and pick up a few groceries. I could make a simple meal. I could talk to people. This does not mean that I did not have panic attacks during the process. Along with days of other debilitating symptoms, such as being in bed for the remainder of the day, isolating myself for days, not going outside, or bathing. But it was a little progress and a small victory, I took it.

One of the symptoms of Bipolar Disorder is mania, where one feels overly confident and excited, and the individual can make impulsive and reckless decisions. In one of my manic moments, I even bought a 400 sq. ft. coffee shop. The funny part looking back, was that 98% of the "customers" were friends who would sit with me. They knew my mental health and did not want me to be alone. The hours were nonexistent. We were open on my "up" days. My friends would call and ask if I was going to be in that day or not prior to opening. I opened when I could, and if the demons became unbearable, I would close the shop, even if it was only an hour later.

In the second phase of my knock-down, a year after being approved for Disability benefits, investigators came to our small town. I was accused of Social Security fraud. After all, they had an undercover camera showing me in the coffee shop "working" and appearing "normal" because mental illness is something "you can see." What is ironic is I remembered that day they were in the shop. I had not been open for several days because of my demons. I may have appeared normal, but I remember having extreme anxiety because none of my friends were in the shop with me. As per usual with my PTSD, I had my exit plan if anything should happen. When they left the shop, I was so worn out from the anxiety and panic attack that I closed and went home.

Despite all the records showing my mental illness was still at the level I qualified for Social Security Disability, the case moved forward. I thought no-big-deal at first because wasn't the point of Social Security Disability to get better if you could?

If you have never found yourself in the trenches of our Justice

System, I will just say that I would not wish it on ANYONE. Every belief you have about our system, criminals, courts and attorneys, are all probably incorrect.

According to PAW Research conducted in 2018 on Federal Conviction Rate in America, once charged with a crime, you only have a 25% chance of regaining your freedom without a conviction.

I took a plea deal. Not the first, second, or third one offered either. The pressure and threats were just too much. Was I mentally competent to make such a decision? Probably not.

I was sentenced to one year and one day for conspiracy to commit mail fraud and immediately remanded into custody. My medications were not given to me because they were not on their approved list. The immediate withdrawals were horrendous. These are medications you are supposed to taper off from. No counseling or mental health services were offered.

Prison turned out to be the biggest blessing in my life. No longer could I run from my thoughts and feelings. No longer could I continue being a prisoner of my mind. I knew I had to get better.

There was a book that changed my life. This was, *You Can Heal Your Life* by Louise Hay, with an accompanying workbook by the same title.

There was a question in the workbook. Basically, it was, do you love or value your life? My immediate answer was 'no'. No, on such a cellular level, it was shocking. Then the follow-up question was: if no, why? The first answer that popped into my mind was I was never taught. My mother showed me on so many occasions just how much my life was really worth. This revelation shocked me to my core. I sat and pondered. That was my turning point in my journey back to health.

I read numerous books, practiced meditation, and dived deep into DBT. I made a decision to stop being the victim and take my power back.

Since my release seven years ago, I continue to stand in my power. Am I 100% better now? I would say yes, but I am sure some of my friends would raise their eyebrows at that. I am the fun, crazy friend where there is always an adventure when you are with me. Don't we all need one of those?

What does all of this have to do with a book on Successonomics, you may ask?

...YOU!

You are the only factor standing between yourself and success.

This past year during the pandemic, how did you react?

- Did you get laid off and could not find another job?
- When you could not find another job, did you park yourself in front of the television, binge-watching Netflix and binge eating junk food?
- Did you start drinking to numb out uncomfortable feelings or to mask the pain?
- Ignore it all, hoping that it would all go away?
- Gain the COVID 20?
- Have a tea party and invite pity?
- Fight with whoever else lives with you?
- Blame everyone for everything?
- Did you say this may be my opportunity to study something I have an interest in?
- Pursue a new career?
- Add new skills to my resume?
- Did you look for a position outside of your comfort zone?
- Did you take care of yourself physically and mentally?

What did you do? This is a good indication of how you handle your life. A Zen Buddhist once said, "How you do anything is how you do everything." You are off to a great start; you picked up a book and took action.

You will never have lasting success until you clean up what is inside of you.

- When is the last time that you really sat down and took an inventory of your life?
- Do you know what really makes you happy?
- How do you feel about your coworkers?
- What do you think about your friendships?
- How do you feel about your intimate relationships?
- How long is your someday list?
- What are the statements you tell yourself that begin with "I am?"

What do you think about the environment you live in?

Wayne Dyer said, "what you think of yourself is what you think of the world." Our environment is a mirror for our internal world and how we see ourselves. Join me on the path to success by finding the answer to these questions. I shared two significant phases of my life to show you the power of our internal dialogue and belief system.

– I had to change my perspective of how I viewed the world.

– I had to stop being a prisoner of my mind and all the limiting beliefs I held about myself.

– I had to stop the complaining and blaming.

– I took responsibility and action to change my world, and you can too.

About Ilya

Ilya Vita is passionate about elevating, empowering, and enlightening the women she works with.

Ilya has been coaching and mentoring for over 15 years. She has worked in career, LGBTQ, women in transition, and crisis coaching. With humor and care Ilya loves to assist people to find their authentic selves and find and achieve what success means to them.

During the 2020/2021 pandemic, Ilya took the opportunity to pursue more training and education. She graduated from Jack Canfield's program *Train The Trainer*, completed RIM Essentials, and received her certification in family, couple, and parent-child coaching.

Ilya is currently completing her training in RIM facilitator, NLP practitioner, and hypnotherapy practitioner. She is a facilitator for an empowerment program for women in prison and halfway houses.

Ilya also launched a podcast called *Legal Pawns* that focuses on advocacy for changes in the legal system.

Ilya started a business called La Bella Vita (The Beautiful Life). It is a place to bring together women of many walks of life to provide a complete healing program. Her global vision is women practicing cooperation, not competition, for the betterment of the world.

Ilya is a transformational specialist. She is a trainer in personal and business achievement, a motivational speaker, and a coach in business, life and relationships.

You can connect with Ilya at:
- Ilya@LaBellaVitaConsultants.com
- LaBellaVitaConsultants.com
- Justice@LegalPawns.org

CHAPTER 11

THE ACCIDENTAL GIFT

BY TERESA MORRIS, DDS

*Gratitude can transform common things into THANKSGIVING,
turn routine jobs into JOY, and change ordinary opportunities
into BLESSINGS.*
~ William A. Ward

"I woke up breathing this morning! I am grateful!"
~ Teresa Morris

The easiest and simplest way to increase the JOY in one's life, to increase one's happiness, health, wealth, and to spread more "love" to one another, is to BE IN GRATITUDE! Being in "gratitude" and staying "present in the moment" is where JOY is found. The past has already passed. The future has no guarantees.

St. Therese of the Child Jesus, Lisieux, France, 1873 – 1897, spoke of praying to God with the heart of a child and putting your trust in God like a child to a Father. God wants all of US to be happy, healthy, and wealthy. The highest compliment we can give God (our Creator) is to be grateful. By being grateful, we show our love of God! And then, there can be a fountain of love that flows into us from God and spills over from us to those around us. By choosing OUR thoughts, from moment to moment, we can change our awareness, and we become in charge of the GRATITUDE we experience. To be in harmony with the frequency of ABUNDANCE, is to BE in the frequency of GRATITUDE! Gratitude is how we access abundance. Gratitude is the highest form of thought.

Gratitude is a CHOICE! One grows in their awareness of the things around themselves to be grateful. Growth will come with mindfulness. Gratitude is a habit that you decide to invest in yourself. Think of gratitude as "praying without ceasing!" "Rejoice always, pray without ceasing, give thanks in all circumstances; for this is the will of God in Christ Jesus for you." 1 Thessalonians 5:16-18, ESV. It is so much about mindfulness and how one looks at things. Is the glass half empty or half full? You admire the bird that sits on your windowsill, or you worry about how to clean the windowsill when the bird leaves. A bill arrives early before your check, you are either grateful it is ready for you when you need it, or you fret about how to pay it early. You either have doubt about your ability to do something, or you just "DO IT ANYWAY," even though you are afraid!

Trusting that everything is how God designed it to be for YOU takes the worry out of circumstances. Philippians 4:6 says, "Do not be anxious about anything, but in every situation, by prayer and petition, with thanksgiving, present your request to God." Be grateful for the moment and what this moment has to offer, and knowing your Lord and your God has something far greater planned for you takes the worry away. This does not mean you accept your circumstances if you dream of different circumstances. Be grateful, but never satisfied. It just means you are grateful for what you have at this moment. By being grateful in the moment, more will be given unto you. Worry gets more worry. Resentment gets you more resentment. Being grateful gets US more to be grateful for. Just as there are many levels of health, there are levels of gratitude. Gratitude, deeply connected with God, is a gratitude that generates more gratitude through abundance, not just through money, our quality of life, the depth of meaning to our life, fulfillment, and OUR aliveness!

Gratitude is a "STATE WE GENERATE!" As we notice more to be grateful for, we generate more gratefulness. Our awareness of the abundance in our life increases. As we pay our bills, being grateful for the money to pay the bill. ...Singing praises to God. As we wash our dishes, being grateful for the dishes to wash. ...Singing praises to God. As we fold our clothes, being grateful for the clothes. ...Singing praises to God. When it rains, being grateful for the roof over our heads, keeping us dry and comfortable. ...Singing praises to God. If you cannot sing, just say a prayer for a loved one while you are doing those chores. No matter what is happening around US.

Once where I worked at night, we had an armed robbery. After our assailant left, our management arrived, and he did not know what to say. He could see the fear and shock on all our faces as we were numb. I spoke up first and said we are grateful no one was hurt or injured. Everyone relaxed at that point. It lifted US all to know we lived through this, and we could all still look each other in the eye. It calmed our nerves. No matter what is happening, we can find something to be grateful for! Sometimes, we must look hard to find something grateful. Do take the time to look! Make it a habit to look for things about which to be grateful!

One way to generate a "state of gratitude" is to be present in the moment. The quickest way to do this is to concentrate on your breathing. Breathe in through your nose, and breathe out through your mouth, as if breathing through a straw. It usually only takes a few breaths to get you into the present moment. Another practice is going about mindless chores.

During my Dental Boards, a classmate and I were discussing over dinner one night, now that we were soon to be dentists, "how much we enjoyed mindless chores!" Mindless chores are activities you do that do not require much thought, like cleaning a toilet, mopping the floors, folding clothes, etc. So what happens when you do these things is you can hum or sing. As you sing along, offer your song to God as prayer. Anything you do, dance, doing yard work, and even making love to your husband! Be grateful! Praise, God!

My belief is that our SOUL is the most important part of our being. We are Human, and we are Soul. Of our life force, our energy, our soul is most important. We are a Soul having a human experience. My Lord and my God is what breathes in me and makes my heart beat. It is called the Autonomous System. It is not under our direct control. God determines when we start living and when we stop. Our breathing and heartbeat are our gifts from God. Because we are made in the likeness of God, our Creator, WE ARE WORTHY!

Our worthiness is given to us at birth by our Creator! Live in gratitude; we are worthy of all the good that WE will allow in our lives. We can put the brakes on the abundance we receive by not believing we are worthy. Everything you have experienced has contributed to who you are now! Embrace the growth that those experiences have contributed.

It is especially important to recognize what we are feeling. How we feel about something is a CHOICE. Often what we are feeling is a learned response. We learned through our family and friends. We must decide from moment to moment what our reaction to a situation will be. A car cuts us off on the highway. We can cuss at the other driver or slow down, be safe, and choose not to react. John Assaraf's *Innersize*, a meditation exercise, in his program, "Winning the Game of Money," reminds us that "we have emotions, we are not our emotions." We decide how we react. We decide how we will feel.

To evolve and grow, one must learn to have control over one's emotions. It is OK to put a reaction on hold – to pause a reaction. This can benefit us in many ways. It gives us time to assess and evaluate. A judgment made too soon may turn out to be an incorrect judgment about a situation. Have you ever walked up to two people already in the middle of a discussion, only to say something inappropriate from an assessment you made about what they were talking about – to have successfully "put your foot into your mouth!"

"Bad things happen to good people" is a theme of M. Scott Peck's book, *People of The Lie*. When the unthinkable happens, we must pause! Wait three days to make a judgment about that situation. Sometimes, it is exceedingly difficult. We must find the BLESSING. There is a lesson for us. There is a gift in every circumstance. God dwells in our hearts! We have the power within us to overcome any hurt or difficulty. A neighbor's son, barely nineteen, was suddenly in a car accident, being placed on life support with no brain activity.

His Mother was understandably in grief in trying to make sense of this event. Consoling her, recommending we wait three days to make a judgment and that we try, as hard as it may seem, to find some good and to find a blessing. Finally, on the third day, when the life support was removed, and he could not breathe on his own – his Mother having given consent – it was found that this young man's body was used to improve and extend the lives of twelve other people through his organ donations. This was a blessing to twelve families! Think of all the lives this young man's life impacted.

Dream building is necessary. Dream building gives you something greater to reach for, to recognize what will really give your life meaning and purpose, so you look forward to waking up with joy in your heart. To truly wake up and love the life you are living is so important! Next, you decide on a plan of action to accomplish your dream. From where you are NOW to where you want to be, is a "gap." It is easy to focus on what you do not have and on the lack of what you desire. By focusing on the gratefulness of where you are at this moment will give you more joy while your goals and dreams are evolving. Emotional maturity is associated with gratitude. There are several action steps one takes to increase the gratitude you experience.

One of the most popular ways is to keep a journal and count your blessings. In the morning, write three to five things for which you are grateful. Begin your sentence with, "I am so grateful and thankful now that _____." Some families I know make this a bedtime ritual with their children.

Simply write a thank you note to someone or mentally send them light and love. This has the benefit of making you happier and strengthening your relationship. Better still, hand-deliver and read it to this person. Set yourself a goal of doing one a month.

Mindful Meditation is another way to increase one's awareness. Without judgment, focus on the present moment. As you sip your morning coffee, be aware of the taste, how it feels for the coffee to go down your throat, the texture, the temperature, etc. Be grateful for the cup, the coffee in the cup, the knowledge you had to make it and all the people it took to produce it, and for all the ways it took to get to your house to fix, the farmer, the pickers, the roasters, the drivers, the packaging companies.

What does Gratitude have in common with the Law of Attraction?

Einstein said, "Everything is energy. That is all there is. Match the frequency of the reality you want, and it cannot help but be yours. This is not philosophy, this is physics." Our BURNING DESIRE and GRATEFUL expectation put us in the frequency that brings it into physical form.

About Teresa

Teresa Faye Morris, DDS, ODCS, BTMP, DBC, LMC, has over 50 years of experience in dentistry, serving dental patients in all capacities – receptionist, dental assistant, dental hygienist, dental lab technician, dentist, and Prosthodontist. Dr. Morris is a Power Client with MGE Management Experts in St Petersburg, Florida, since 2014. On a trip to Spain, visiting Madrid, Segovia, and Avila, she had a "spiritual awakening" and decided to become a Discalced Carmelite, laity. This decision required her to practice the Catholic faith. At that time, she was a Christian, but Protestant. She was able to marry spirituality with religion.

For the next five years, she studied with Carmelite Friars in a Monastery in Garland, Texas. Several visits into her study, her flight being late, entered through the kitchen, one of her favorite places to socialize. She studied classic spirituality, and one Buddhist Monk resided at the Monastery. One of her favorite places for retreats was Lebh Shomea in Sarita, Texas. One of any faith may stay for any length of time; the only requirement is to enter in silence and have daily communion.

Dr. Morris's studies include many Mentors – Mary Morrissey, Matthew Boggs, Jennifer Joy Jimenez, John Boggs, Kirsten Wells, Rich Boggs, Jack Canfield, Patty Aubrey, Zig Ziglar, Wayne Dyer, Bob Proctor, Les Brown, John Assaraf, Natalie Ledwell, and Eddie Sergey.

Dr. Morris is an accomplished scuba diver and underwater photographer, but has retired from actively teaching PADI, Master Scuba Diver Training Programs, and her Certification included 15 Specialties. In order to advance her skills in Tech Diving, she was certified in Cave Diving by Steve Gerrard of Akumal, Mexico. Other interests include gardening, biking, hiking, boating (motor and sail), paddleboard, kayak, roller skating, pool, and bowling. She would find it difficult to sit for a game of bridge or dominoes.

Her focus now is teaching Transformational Principals in Health, Fitness, Time & Money Freedom, and Relationships, helping younger dentists reactivate their patients through social media platforms, and entering her first body-building competition.

CHAPTER 12

BE YOUR BETTER SELF

BY EMIGDIO M. ARIAS

Towards the end of 2009, I created some undesired outcomes in my life because I was being myself. I had a political falling-out with my boss at the time and the organization with whom I was employed. Right around the same time, problems were beginning to surface in my marriage and in my family. The stress and anxiety from these situations also began to affect my health in a negative way...all because I was being myself.

At the time, I felt that I hit rock bottom, and there was so much doubt, worry and uncertainty regarding whether I would recover and bounce back. In the past, whenever I would find myself in an undesirable situation, I would always resort to praying. This is when I would beg and plead with God to save me, protect me, and make everything better. However, nothing was getting better. I felt that I fell out of God's favor and that I finally dug myself into a hole so deep that not even He could get me out. Being myself, I allowed anger, sadness, fear, hurt and guilt to occupy my mind, so that it became too difficult for me to connect with the One who always protected me.

I remember saying to myself, "Emigdio, you really did it now! You've managed to screw up every area of your life—your career, your family, your health, and now God's ignoring you, too!"

123

Being myself, I blamed my former boss, my former colleagues, my wife, my parents and anyone else I could blame for where my life was. I even blamed God. Being myself, I wanted revenge. I wanted to get even. I wanted to retaliate. I wanted them to hurt like I was hurting. I was in so much pain, I wanted everyone to feel that same pain.

Being myself, I believed I was the victim. I justified my part in co-creating the undesirable situations. I convinced myself that I had to do what I had to do, and that everyone else was wrong. Things were far from getting better. They were actually becoming worse as each day went by.

I couldn't eat. I couldn't sleep, and I would just smoke cigarette after cigarette to pass the time. Being myself, I robbed myself of peace of mind, sleep, love, laughter, joy and inspiration. Because I was in my own head, because I was in my own way, and because I was being myself, living was no longer desirable to me.

The situation only became worse as I continued being myself. The more things got worse, the more difficult it became for me to go on.

Why does being yourself create the opposite of what you want? Why is it extremely important to stop being yourself to create better outcomes to improve your situation? Why is it that you can actually open the door to create the life you want, once you stop being yourself?

Your beliefs, thoughts, self-talk, words and actions created the undesirable outcomes in your life. Being yourself consists of all of those things. In order to change your situation and create your desired outcomes, you must change yourself—meaning you must let go of all of the limiting beliefs and decisions that no longer serve you and replace them with beliefs that do. You must change your thinking to only focus on what you want—what you really want. Your inner dialogue or self-talk must be inspiring, motivating, empowering and positive rather than destructive. The words you speak are magical and create your life, so every word you speak must be spoken in a way that affirms what you truly want and how you want your life to be. Every action that you take must reflect a step towards creating the life you truly desire.

What is it that you must become to stop being yourself? What does this look like? What does this sound like? What does this feel like? What is it that you need to become to only create your desired outcomes and to create the life you truly desire? The only way to stop being yourself is to become YOUR BETTER SELF. I will go as far as to say that you need to become your BEST SELF, however, this is achieved by constant and continuous self-improvement during the course of one's life. So, start by becoming your Better Self, but always aiming to become your Best Self.

- *How do you become your Better Self?*

- *How is this accomplished?*

- *How is this achieved?*

- *How do you know when you have become your Better Self?*

1. **First, you can start by taking 100% responsibility for your life.**

You need to accept responsibility for all that has been created and all that has been manifested in your life. This is where you stop blaming others and outside circumstances and events for how your life is at this time. This is where you make the connection unconsciously to be aware of it consciously, that your present life is a direct result of your beliefs, thoughts, self-talk, words and actions. I plead with you to stay away from blaming yourself and raking yourself over the coals. Accepting responsibility and faulting yourself are two entirely different things. As you accept responsibility, also accept that you are not your behavior, and that you are doing your best with the resources you have available. This is true now and was true in the past. As time goes on, you acquire more resources and are able to make better decisions that reflect being your Better Self.

Being your Better Self allows you to achieve personal power. Accepting 100% responsibility for your life is the tool necessary to realizing you have the power to create the life you truly desire. This is where the victim, the old you, disappears. This is where you stop being YOUR OLD SELF to become YOUR BETTER SELF.

2. Next is FORGIVENESS:

You can start with forgiving yourself which you have already started doing as I shared with you a hidden gem a few sentences ago. Again, you are not your behaviors and you are doing your best with the resources you have available. Whatever you did in the past, just know that you were not that behavior. Wherever you may have fallen short or missed the mark in the past, always remember that you were doing your best with the resources you had at the time. You deserve to be forgiven. However, how can you expect anyone to forgive you if you haven't forgiven yourself? To be your Better Self today and in the future, you must put the old self and all that was done in the past behind you. Your Better Self is only dedicated to creating the life you really want with your new resources.

As you forgive yourself, it will be much easier to forgive others because you will make the connection unconsciously and be aware of it consciously, that they (the others) are not their behaviors, and that they were doing their best with the resources they had available. This is when you become grateful for them and the role they played in your life that created the opportunity for you to learn, heal and become your Better Self. Your Better Self will realize and know that they deserve forgiveness just like you do. Whatever you desire for yourself—desire it for them as well. Wish them happiness, health, wealth, success and prosperity. What you wish for others you also wish for yourself. Remember that famous saying, "Be careful what you wish for" and replace it with, "Be careful what you wish for others!"

3. Now, REMOVE ALL OBSTACLES IN YOUR WAY and TAKE ACTION!

Know who you want to become, what you want to accomplish, what you want to achieve, what you want to get and what you want to experience. Only focus on your desired outcomes! Any belief and emotion that isn't in alignment with what you want and doesn't support your getting it is an obstacle. When you are definite and passionate about your purpose, you must know that the Universe wants all of this for you as well, and will conspire in every way to make your goals and dreams manifest into reality. When a young child picks something up from the floor and begins to put it in their mouth, usually we hear the child's parent say, "Put that down! You don't know where that came from!" Utilize this metaphor whenever a belief or emotion surfaces that doesn't support you achieving what you want. Close your eyes, and visualize your Creator saying to you, "Put that down! You don't know where that belief or emotion came from!"

The Universe <u>always</u> rewards action, ALWAYS! The only way to manifest what we want on the physical plane is to take action. Every day is an opportunity to do something that supports your goals. When we take action and only focus on our desired outcomes we will create exactly what those are. When we train our mind to do this, we leave absolutely no room to focus on what we don't want, therefore leaving no possibility to create an undesired outcome. Your Better

Self understands this, and your Better Self knows this. We only live once in this body, and in this lifetime. Be your Better Self, aim high and go after what you really want.

What if you accepted 100% responsibility for your life? What if you forgave yourself and others? What if you removed all obstacles and TAKE ACTION? What would happen if you didn't?

During that difficult time in my life, I heard the words that would change my life forever..."Your life is a direct result of your beliefs, thoughts, self-talk, words and actions." At that moment, I made the connection between all of these and what manifested in my life. I saw the reflections. I saw the projections.

The world around me was a mirror reflecting all that was happening inside of me. I was a movie projector, and what was on the film was being projected on to the outside world. I control what's on the film, and if I don't like the movie being played, all I have to do is change the film. I am responsible for what I believe, what I think about, what I say to myself, the words I speak and the things I do. This is when I achieved Personal Power. From this moment on, I was going to be in control of my movie.

Accepting 100% responsibility for my life and its outcomes was and continues to be the most empowering feeling I have ever experienced. I no longer identified as a victim. I made the connection that thoughts are things, and my thoughts are creating my life. I realized that I created all of the undesirable outcomes which manifested in my life. I was so grateful for that because that insight indicated to me that I can also create the outcomes I truly desire, if I only focused on them.

It was time to change what was on my film. I identified all of the beliefs I had that were limiting my growth and preventing me from achieving what I wanted. Even though this wasn't easy, a deep sense of gratitude appeared as I realized that I acquired a majority of these beliefs from my childhood. They weren't mine. They never were. I picked them up from all of my earliest teachers such as my parents, close family members, the priests from the church I attended as a kid, my grade school teachers, and from things I watched and listened to on television.

As I let these beliefs go, I adopted new ones such as knowing that I was created with a specific purpose in mind, and that God's desire for me is to be happy, healthy, wealthy, successful and prosperous.

I started to have fun with forgiveness. I forgave myself for anything and everything. I forgave anyone and everyone—just because. As the days went by, it became a challenge to identify anyone else to forgive because I went through my list thoroughly and let go of all the anger, sadness, fear, hurt and guilt. As I released all of these people, I released myself as well. I said to myself, "I am free. I'm finally free".

Letting go of the limiting beliefs and releasing the negative emotions from my mind and body allowed me to gain absolute clarity. I wrote down what I wanted and how I wanted my life to be. I made a promise to myself to only focus on my desired outcomes and to take action daily to create my life with intention.

Eleven years later, I'm doing what I absolutely love and enjoy, and earning more money than I ever have. I feel better and look better than when I was in my twenties. My relationships are with people I choose to have them with – where there is respect, appreciation and gratitude. My connection with my Higher Self is powerful— where I know that I am always being guided, protected and lead to my highest good.

Here is a summary of my aims and desires for you:

> (i) To take your personal and professional success to the next level.

(ii) To have you aim high and go after what you want.

(iii) To strive to help you and others to lead happier, healthier, and wealthier lives.

(iv) To accelerate your path to a Triumphant Mindset.

Once you achieve your goals, create new ones.

Always have something to look forward to!

About Emigdio

Emigdio M. Arias is an Elite-Level Mindset Coach, Success Coach, Executive Coach, NLP Trainer, and Personal Transformation and Thought Leader, he will help you or your organization achieve higher levels of success.

Emigdio is the CEO of Triumphant Mindset, LLC., where he facilitates greater success for individuals and groups to get from where they are to where they want to be.

For over twenty years, he has had a passion for helping people and creating better leaders. He focuses on a transformational process, utilizing techniques that have helped thousands of people achieve their personal and professional goals. With a strong background in NLP, Success Principles, Hypnotherapy, and Time Line Therapy®, he provides personalized training that helps people gain critical insights, take risks, and overcome challenges.

An energetic, engaging presenter and empathetic, yet bold communicator, he helps improve communications at companies across industries – assisting people in discovering opportunities for personal and professional development, making organizations stronger and more capable of realizing aggressive business goals.

Professional Credentials:
- Certified NLP Trainer
- Certified Master NLP Coach
- Trainer in Hypnotherapy
- Certified Executive Coach
- Certified Canfield Success Principles Trainer
- Certified Master Practitioner in Time Line Therapy®

Emigdio M. Arias helps individuals and groups let go of limiting beliefs and release negative emotions—increasing productivity and happiness. He helps in goal identification and goal setting—providing creative, effective solutions to elicit transformative breakthroughs.

Emigdio helps propel people to define their purpose, take 100% responsibility for their lives, and take inspired action to go after what they really want.

Emigdio proposes:
- Are you ready to take your personal and professional success to the next level?
- Aim high. Go after what you want.
- He strives to help people lead happier, healthier, and wealthier lives.
- Connect with him today to accelerate your path to a Triumphant Mindset.

Contact information for Emigdio:
- Email: info@TriumphantMindset.com
- Info@EmigdioArias.com
- Instagram: @triumphant.mindset
- www.TriumphantMindset.com
- www.EmigdioArias.com

CHAPTER 13

EMPOWERING YOUR WAY TO EMOTIONAL FREEDOM

BY KIM SILVERMAN

My biggest secret to success was learned during the most tragic time in my life.

Before discovering that my healthy, energetic husband had terminal brain cancer, I believed I had everything. I was with the love of my life. We had a successful, thriving business, a beautiful home, two wonderful children, and two lovable dogs—the dream many Americans strive to achieve. It never occurred to me that we wouldn't grow old together.

His death, and my grief, made me realize how dependent I was on him. When I say I was devastated, that would be an understatement. I was totally consumed and shocked by the enormity of the situation, and that threw me into mind and body overload. Literally, I shut down into a numbing void where I was no longer connected to my emotions. It was through grief counseling that I began to understand how I had buried my emotions so deep that when the emotional reservoir was re-opened, they flooded in like a tsunami. From that point on, my emotions began ruling my day-to-day life. I was engulfed by them. Finally, I realized that I needed to learn how to ride the wave of my emotions rather than be consumed by them.

Empowerment came to me in the most unexpected way. We humans are trained to believe that healing and transformation is a long and difficult process. But in reality it can be quickly attained. Returning to emotional freedom can be powerfully achieved by first focusing on your breath, then by giving your body permission to feel the emotion in the moment, and then releasing it to allow a more positive feeling to enter.

I never imagined that my soulmate's passing would help me show up bigger and brighter in the world, like a phoenix rising from the ashes. My pain awakened me to my life purpose as a healer, propelling me from a 30+ year career in finance to working as a Certified Life Coach and Clinical Hypnotherapist. By following that new desire within me, I opened the doors to learning how to intentionally manage my own emotions.

Through my own experiences of healing and my training as a coach and hypnotherapist, I've learned that focused and rhythmic breathing can be a powerful tool to help clients tune into their subconscious mind to manage their emotions, so they are fueled by them rather than paralyzed. It is the subconscious mind—where we house our thoughts, emotions, and feelings—that is responsible for delivering those images to our conscious mind and those sensations to our body, resulting in an enhanced life experience. And that same subconscious mind is fed this information by our higher self.

I wish I had known then what I know now—that allowing the emotion to express itself, breathe through it, release it and then ask for a new, better feeling to fill the mind and body—is key to transforming your pain into emotional freedom and empowerment.

I teach my clients, who are often in a state of grief—whether it be over a death, a job loss, or a relationship—how to work through various stages and cycles of emotions such as numbness, sadness, anger, anxiety, and depression. I help them learn various coping tools and often start with one of my breathing techniques to initiate the process of managing their emotions to return to a place of peace and calm.

By starting with the focus on breathing, this interrupts and unlocks the brain patterns and allows clients to tune out the distractions around them and focus inwardly. This inward focus begins the process of listening to their inner guidance, which is key to their success in manifesting anything they want to achieve.

There are four breathing techniques that I use for different situations, for myself and my clients.

FOUR BREATHING TECHNIQUES:

1. The Attention Grabber

This technique is perfect for when anyone is experiencing sheer panic/anxiety attacks or full-body fear, and their mind can't think of anything else at that moment. When they want to regain control over their mind and body and bring it back to a calm and relaxed state, I recommend The Attention Grabber.

Technique:
Rapid Breath in
Rapid Breath out
Rapid Breath in
Rapid Breath out
Rapid Breath in
Rapid Breath out
Long Slow Breath in – 2 – 3 – 4
Long Slow Breath out – 2 – 3 – 4
Repeat three times or as many times as needed.

If this breathing technique has worked for you, then you will feel calmer and more centered and be able to focus more clearly.

2. The Box Breath

Some people also refer to this method as the Four-Square Breathing or Controlled Breathing. I refer to it as the Box Breath. This technique is universally used to gain control over your emotions and return you back to a state of calm. You can also start using this method after you have successfully completed The Attention Grabber technique. Your mind needs to be under your control for this technique to be the most effective, which is why doing The Attention Grabber technique first is important for runaway minds.

The Box Breath is my favorite for life situations that have caused me or clients to feel anxious, worried, or stressed. The box breath, using a four-count, allows us to quickly let go of those unwanted emotions and return to a state of calmness and peace. I have had many clients say that this is also their favorite "go-to" breathing technique to let go of stress and fear.

Technique:
> Breathe in – 2 – 3 – 4
> Hold – 2 – 3 – 4
> Breathe out – 2 – 3 – 4
> Hold – 2 – 3 – 4
> Repeat three times or as many times as needed.

3. Quick Exhale Breath

This technique is great for resetting your mindset. For example, this is perfect if you're changing from one task to another at work, feeling annoyed at someone, or have been asked to do something that you don't want to do.

Technique:
> Long deep inhale – 2 – 3 – 4
> Quick exhale out
> Repeat three times or as many times as needed.

Success with this technique allows you to move on without judgment.

4. Deep Meditation Breath

I often use this technique to begin a guided meditation, which helps create a deep relationship with you and your mind and body. The breath is key to making that connection to your higher self. People who enjoy meditating usually have their own unique way of beginning the session. To begin meditating, I find a quiet place where I won't be disturbed and where I feel at ease. Some people like to use candles and music. I prefer silence so I can focus on this next deep breathing technique.

Technique:
      Long deep inhale 2 – 3 – 4
      Slow long exhale 2 – 3 – 4 – 5 – 6
      Repeat three times or as many times as needed.

Having these breathing techniques is the first step I've used for myself and my clients to get present with the mind and body. Now, when life throws a curveball, and we feel an emotional reaction that does not feel good—such as anger, fear, or sadness—I use one of the above breathing techniques to kick off my next process called "STOP, DROP and ROLL," which helps restore calm and peace.

I have adapted this concept from my childhood teachings by our firefighters, who taught us to Stop, Drop and Roll if we smelled smoke in our room. The adaptation has also been inspired by Christy Whitman and the Quantum Council's teachings. I now use it as a hypnotherapy technique to help clients gain an awareness of their emotions, to release that emotion and then to bring in a new emotion that feels in alignment with their body.

PROCESS: THE STOP, DROP AND ROLL TO ZEN:

A. STOP – When clients feel stressed or fearful (or something else), I instruct them to stop (this interrupts the recurring brain patterns) and start one of my breathing techniques above to bring focused attention on the emotion that is forthcoming.

After that, I invite them to bring awareness to the discordant emotion that they are feeling. I remind them they don't have to live with this discomfort and that they have the power to change this emotion to something that feels better.

B. DROP – Next, I ask them to close their eyes and drop their attention inward, focusing on the emotion that is coursing through their body. I have them give this emotion full permission to express itself in their body. The key here is to not be afraid of feeling the emotion, whatever it might be. Instead, the key is to embrace it and appreciate that it has caught their attention so that it can now be released.

The good news is that they don't have to name the emotion or go into the story behind it. They just have to focus on the energy of the emotional wave coursing through their body.

Emotions often feel like a wave, and I show clients how to ride the wave until it eventually dissipates. Often there is one wave after another as each rhythmically peaks and valleys before the next one begins right behind it. Sometimes it takes a while, and at other times, it is very quick. It really depends on how deeply ingrained the emotion is in the body and memory.

C. ROLL out – Once they are fully embodying that emotion, I then have them instruct their body to "roll out" of this unwanted feeling.

Sometimes with clients, I'll use the imagery of pulling a plug from the base of their spine and draining out the energy. Or they can imagine filling a bubble of light with this emotion and setting it free to drift away. A favorite image is to imagine a large set of loving hands being extended in front of them, ready to receive anything that my client is ready to let go of. I then have my clients envision pulling out this energetic emotion from their body and handing it over to the hands that gladly take it away. It does not matter what imagery is used, and the client can be as creative as they want to be in that moment. This frees them of the concern that they might be doing it "wrong." More importantly, it gives them an unhindered freedom to do what feels right for them.

D. ROLL in – When the emotional wave is no longer strong and present, I ask clients to decide what emotion they would rather feel. They look for a better feeling emotion and imagine filling their body with a bright light containing that emotional essence. I then ask them to imagine "rolling in" or bringing that new essence completely into their body. If they have difficulty accessing this new emotion, I will invite them to think of a time in the past when they felt that better feeling. If they have never experienced it before, then they can imagine what it could feel like or think of someone who is living the inspirational life they want to experience.

Before ending this exercise, I will have them check in with their body to determine if it is feeling lighter than before. I ask them to allow enough time and compassion for their body to return to a state of peace and calm, reminding themselves that it is okay to have felt those uncomfortable emotions. I invite them to be grateful that the emotion made itself known so that they could process it out of their mind and body.

Often during this STOP, DROP and ROLL process, clients or

I will get clarity on what transpired. Sometimes I will see that I was over-reacting to my own situation or that a client needed to release an old emotion stemming from their childhood that wasn't fully processed and resolved.

When we hold onto the emotion without releasing it, we begin to attract and manifest more of the same through the Law of Attraction, where "like attracts like," whether good or bad. Plus, holding onto unhealthy emotions often results in wear-and-tear on our bodies and sometimes leads to illness.

In my own life, I have found it vital to always try to find the silver lining and the blessings from these emotional traumas. Grief is not linear and I still have my moments of feeling the loss. Reframing my suffering to discover the learning has helped me attain my emotional freedom.

The more I have practiced these processes and techniques, the more proficient I have become in managing my happiness. I am now able to shift my emotional state of mind and body from feeling bad to better in just a matter of minutes.

These techniques have become important tools of transformation for clients looking to create a more successful life—whatever that means for them. Success is unique to each individual and might mean living a life of happiness to one person, or financial freedom to another, and spiritual connectedness to yet another. For me, success is living a life of peace and happiness, and making a positive impact on the world through my healing work. I'm so thankful that I have the opportunity to help others transform, so they too can make the world a better place in their own way!

About Kim

Kim Silverman is a Certified Clinical Hypnotherapist, Master Law of Attraction Coach and Quantum Energy Master.

Some people have dubbed Kim, "the Law of Attraction Hypnotherapist," as she has helped her clients release the negative emotions that block them from attracting what they desire. She enjoys helping people let go of the unconscious reasons that have chained them to repeating unwanted patterns of behavior.

Kim specializes in helping people let go of stress and anxiety to return to a calm and relaxed state. She has found that when her clients can intentionally quiet their mind and body, they can think more clearly, tap into their intuition, and activate their creative thinking to solve problems or make key decisions.

Kim received her Bachelor of Science degree in Business from the University of Colorado, Boulder. She started her professional career as a Certified Public Accountant (CPA) and enjoyed a 30+ year career in executive finance roles with various companies.

Through healing from her husband's death, she found her new career and life purpose as a Certified Life Coach and Clinical Hypnotherapist. She has guided many through their transformational shift to make life-altering changes and thrive in their own purpose. Kim holds certifications from the Quantum Success Coaching Academy, The Institute for Transpersonal Studies, and the Law of Attraction Life Coach Academy.

You can connect with Kim at:
- Website: www.kimsilvermantransformation.com
- Linked In: www.linkedin.com/in/kimsilverman0
- Instagram: www.instagram.com/kimsilvermantransformation
- Twitter: www.twitter.com/KimSilvermanTr
- Facebook: www.facebook.com/kimsilvermantransformation

CHAPTER 14

HOPE IS A NARROW BLADE OF GRASS

BY KANDIEE CAMPBELL

Have you ever thought about what life would be like if you hadn't been born? That was a thought that had rolled around in my head since I was a child. Growing up, I thought I had a decent life. I was fortunate to have experiences that many just dream about. I have lived all over the world and seen and had opportunities that many could only wish to have. From the outside view, I had a good life. Deep down inside, I was falling apart.

When I was five, I had an unfortunate experience at my grandmother's ranch. She had a pond that was about 15 feet deep and had fish, geese, and ducks. It was murky water that always scared me because I could not see the bottom. One day, while outside, I was leaning over the pond, and I fell into the murky water. I could not swim, as I had flunked swimming in the ocean while living in Greece. I bobbed up and down and struggled to keep my head above water. I was finally able to hold myself up enough to scream for help. When my mom and my grandmother heard my scream, they came running out of the house and pulled me to safety. I was grasping a small blade of grass that somehow was keeping me afloat. I do not know how as it was not strong enough to hold any weight. To this day, I feel as though angels were holding me up. This was the beginning of my journey of wondering why I came into the world.

My life growing up seemed normal. I had the same struggles as most kids and really didn't think too much of it. The part that was different was I been pushed to grow up quicker than I was prepared for. This part I did know was not normal. I was an only child, and my parents did not have the best communications skills. My mother really did not have other adults to confide in. Since I was the only one my mother was around a lot, I became the confidant at the early age of three. I took in all the adult problems that my father should have been talking to her about. As I got older, my parents' problems got worse, and I was in the middle. This had a huge impact on my life.

I was wanting to escape all the pain I was feeling. The pain required attention, and I just wanted it to go away. Pain occurs for a reason; many people try to ignore it and shove it down. I was good at that. This pain would follow me throughout my life. It affected my relationships, my marriage, and even my self-confidence. Deep inside, the pain was like a volcano just bubbling and waiting. I had so much just shoved down it did not take much for it to start overflowing. For many years, it was not pretty. I had anger, sadness, and plain hurt that my inner child was needing to heal. It would begin to come out, and I would again shove it down. I did not take 100 percent responsibility for my life, and it would get much worse before it got better. I had faulty thinking, and I did not realize or even acknowledge it.

I was an active-duty military spouse and had two wonderful boys. Life took me on many adventures and many moves. From the outside, my life looked stable. All along, I presented as if everything was okay. Therefore, these pains remained buried.

I could only run so far and bury the hurt. I convinced myself I was okay, and I could keep going on the path that I was on. I had managed to build a strong wall around myself, which kept love and pain out, or at least, so I thought. Again, my thinking was faulty. I was progressing with life. I was still always wondering what my purpose was; why I was still here. I would even repress those thoughts. I was determined that no one was going to hurt me anymore; as it turns out, I was hurting myself the most. Believe me when I say you can run from others hurting you, but if you are the one inflicting the pain, there is no escape.

My inner critic was always speaking to me and would tell me how wrong I was, reminding me of what I should or could have done or regrets for what I did. My inner critic was getting louder, and the more I ran, the more fear I experienced. My inner critic had even convinced me not to trust myself or my intuition. By not trusting my intuition, I had made some bad choices and was having to live with the outcomes. I struggled with making the simplest of decisions without second-guessing myself. I had become very good at being a people pleaser, and I had become co-dependent.

I would go on to get a bachelor's, two master's degrees and work on a doctorate, and using certifications trying to soothe the pain. Life kept moving along. My life appeared okay; then the bottom fell out. In a matter of years, I lost both of my parents within 18 months of each other, and I had a business fail and relationship problems. I developed health issues and lost my four-month-old. This was the last straw. I was hurting even more and struggling to contain the pain now. I fell into a pit of depression and found myself crying out to God to let me go. I wanted so much for this pain to cease and to leave this life. My life was at the bottom, and I could no longer deny the pain nor shove it down.

While I was crying out and asking for my life to end, I heard in my ears, "No, you have more work to do." When I listened to this voice, I reacted with anger. I had so much pain, and I was being told I could not end my life. At the same time, I had this nudging that kept prompting me to acknowledge I had to change. I felt a yearning deep inside that wanted to find a solution to heal the embedded pain deep inside of me. I was at the bottom and realized the only direction I could go was up, and I had to find a solution to change my life.

I remember hearing my mother on her death bed having a bunch of regrets. She regretted not following her dreams and allowing her fears to get in the way of her truly living. I realized I did not want to come to the end of my life and have all these regrets about what I did or didn't do. I was getting ready to have a significant birthday, and I wanted to find a way to change my life and even someone else's life before too much life passed them by. I started my journey of finding how to soothe my inner ache.

I found a program that helped me to see all the negative energy that I had created and which I was carrying with me everywhere I went. I learned to clear energy, and I began to understand that we always are making choices, and I had a choice to improve my life or stay the same.

I learned that I needed to take responsibility for all the experiences in my life, both the good and bad. I learned from a mentor that I needed to take a deep dive into my embedded pain in order to heal. My mentor helped me realize I had a pattern of self-defeating habits of blaming, complaining, and listening to my inner critic. I learned to give myself a tiny bit of compassion. With help, I began to realize I was making choices, and if I wanted a different outcome, I needed to change my response to the events occurring in and around me.

I also started to tap into all the years of my psychology education. I had furthered my education to try to find solutions for my own pain. However, I had not tapped into all that I had learned. It took me being at 'rock bottom' to realize that I had all the tools and strategies; I just needed to implement them.

I began to pay attention to the words I was telling myself because those words affected my thoughts. I developed the habit of pausing when my inner critic would begin talking and then reframe my thoughts about what I was thinking. I established the habit of writing letters to my inner child and giving her a voice when she was fearful. I would do EFT (Emotional Freedom Technique) to help calm down my nervous system and deactivate the sympathetic nervous system (flight-or-fight) mode. Once I activated my parasympathetic nervous system, I was able to have clearer thoughts and arrive at solutions that were more effective.

Many people function with low or depleted levels of neurotransmitters. They are necessary to promote happiness. I was one of those individuals who functioned with crashing or low levels, and I was not happy, nor did I function well.

Serotonin is an endorphin that helps people remain positive and not be worried. When we are worried, obsessive, or even irritable, this can indicate depleted serotonin levels. I went far too long without sufficient levels. Even when we are not getting enough sleep, this can affect our serotonin levels. When I acknowledge and praise myself for my small wins, I build my serotonin levels, and that makes me feel good.

Catecholamines, better known as norepinephrine, dopamine, and adrenaline, help to keep you alert and energized. When those neurotransmitters are crashing, that is when you experience lethargy or a funk. I admit I walked around in a funk more than I care to think of. Now I know my catecholamines are sufficient because I feel energized. When I am energized, I am able to accomplish more things and make beneficial choices.

The final neurotransmitter is GABA (gamma-aminobutyric acid). This endorphin is responsible for feeling relaxed or stress-free. When we are feeling overwhelmed or stressed, we are probably deficient in GABA. I existed for many years with depleted GABA levels. Higher levels of stress can affect our cortisol which is a hormone that puts us into fight-or-flight mode. Even a perceived stressor can create this cycle.

Whenever I begin to feel I am slipping into a slump, I change my state by dancing around for two minutes, and I sing out loud. It is amazing what body movement does for the release of neurotransmitters for happiness, such as serotonin, catecholamines, and GABA (gamma-aminobutyric acid). Exercising can boost your levels and is quite beneficial. So anytime you find yourself in a funk, get up and move. Go dance, run, take a walk. You will notice an improvement in your state.

Now, when I find myself becoming stressed, I pause; then I begin to ask myself what am I thinking? Then I work on changing my thoughts or tweak the words I am telling myself. If I have lots of time, I will begin to quiet my mind by meditation. I have found meditation to be so helpful. I usually begin with this before I assess my thoughts. I can have clearer thoughts after meditation.

It's important to listen to our bodies. Our body will tell us what it needs, and we have just gotten out of the habit of listening. Many of us are so busy doing that we don't take the time to listen to what our body is telling us what it wants or needs. When we neglect to listen, we open ourselves to all sorts of health issues. I developed serious health issues because I chose not to listen to my body. It has been an arduous journey to change, but it is changing, and my doctor is amazed.

So, if you find yourself falling into a slump and not liking the direction you are heading, remember to always question it and do the following:

1. Question your thoughts – If you cannot calm your thoughts, begin to meditate, and your mind will begin to quiet.
2. If you experience depressing thoughts – Change your physical state and get moving.
3. Always listen to your body – Our bodies talk to us and give us clues when it needs attention. If we ignore it, we often have to pay severe consequences.
4. Always take ownership of your feelings and thoughts – We are responsible for how we choose to feel or what we think.

I am still a work in progress, but I am much farther along than I was a week ago and even this time last year. I learned that I had to take complete ownership of my feelings and thoughts. As I did this, my life began to change for the better, and it led me to a more fulfilling life, which I love. Maybe those angels that held up that five-year-old clinging for life hold me up today—maybe just manifesting differently.

When we listen and make choices that serve us,
our lives can be everything we desire.

About Kandiee

Kandiee Campbell is a transformational leader and coach, energy reader, and certified "Happy for No Reason" Trainer. Kandiee became a "Happy for No Reason" Trainer because she wanted to learn skills that would enable her to live a happy and fulfilled life no matter what life throws at you. Kandiee desires people to live free and not feel insignificant.

Kandiee works with women who have experienced a traumatic event that has left them feeling isolated, confused, or less than their true selves. She helps them uncover hidden emotional triggers that keep them stuck and playing small. She helps them create a plan for moving forward so that they can be set free from the self-defeating patterns that hold them back, and learn to feel happy and in control no matter what life throws at them.

Kandiee has an M.A. in Clinical Psychology and counseling from the University of the Rockies, and an M.Ed. in Educational Technology from the University of Maryland. Kandiee is in pursuit of her Doctorate in Clinical Psychology. Kandiee has co-authored papers for the Hawaii Psychological Association on "A Call to Managing Serious Mental Health Risks Among Pretraining Military Recruits."

Kandiee has additional training in trauma recovery and helps people make peace with early childhood trauma they have encountered. She has a black belt in Tae Kwon Do. Kandiee loves to create gourmet food for her family and friends and loves gourmet cooking and baking. She lives in Ewa Beach, Hawaii, with her family and two rescue dogs. Kandiee has traveled to over 40 countries and lived in seven. Kandiee has enjoyed the experience of exposure to many different cultures.

CHAPTER 15

THE ABUNDANT LIFE

BY ROSIE GREGERSON SCHUELLER

When you have an idea to create a new way, a new product, a new process, and people tell you it will not work that way, remember maybe no one has tried it this way before. Think big, better yet…think HUGE!

Never settle for small or less. The world is full of abundance and blessings. You just need to find them, cultivate them, and share them. That is the key for me, share my blessings. I know how to create abundance—you have to share. Things, knowledge, money are not meant to be hoarded, but shared. I believe one of the reasons people experience lack and have scarcity is they are not cultivating their blessings.

Just as a seed is just a seed until it is planted, watered, and pollinated to produce its bounty, it must still give back some of its seeds to the earth to continue to survive.

I am a real estate broker and building contractor, Canfield Certified Trainer, and a Christian. I know how neglected and abandoned homes can hurt a neighborhood and community. People start to feel trapped by their surroundings devalue their property and the neighborhood actually gets sick, depressed, and desperate, and the community mindset becomes one of lack and survival.

What if people all worked together? Imagine the possibilities. Some people have the gift of vision. Some are planners and schedulers. Some are handy people who, when shown how can truly be amazing at fixing things. It is amazing what the internet has done to show us how to do and fix almost anything.

Many people ask me how I got to where I am, having a lifestyle friendly real estate business, and the 'how' and 'why' I became a building contractor and a Realtor. The answer is, I have a vision. I see a vacant house in poor condition, and I can imagine it repaired, cleaned, and alive again with the hope of a family enjoying it. How did I reach this goal? Pure grit, faith, and not being afraid of hearing no. I also have rental property that brings in a nice source of passive income.

I have built several homes in addition to the real estate that I purchased, remodeled, and sold. I grew up in a nice suburb of the twin cities and attended a great high school where I was able to learn how to plan, delegate and host many events as a member of the student council for approximately 1800 students. I would be much older when I came to appreciate the value of learning to be a leader that I developed back then.

After college at the University of Wisconsin, I received my bachelor's and continued on to graduate school for my MBA. I worked for a big-box electronic company in their corporate office as a buyer of personal computers and printers. I was an intricate part of launching Windows 95, helping to grow the chain from 96 to over 300 stores. When I left, one of two computers in the world were purchased from our stores. After health issues and life changes, I went to work for our family's business.

My parents owned and managed apartments buildings in the Minneapolis area. I would work for them in some capacity from the 1980s to my Father's death in 2013. During this time, I worked at the properties renting, marketing, and doing collections. I learned so many things about customer service, property maintenance, and how to assign and delegate tasks. I still remember my Dad saying if you are going to have rental properties, keep them close together so as to share staff and build up. Better to have one large building boiler vs. one boiler in every single-family home rental. The same footprint of land can have many units if built-up vs. having to pay for and maintain single-family rental home lots. The advantages of multi-housing were apparent.

Many people are currently defaulting into the negative right now, but who can blame them. We all really need a warm hug and a pep talk. I cannot help the whole world, but I may be able to touch a few, and hopefully, they will help a few and there will be a domino effect – which can be exponential. If 2020 taught me anything, it is how fast and wide disease can travel. Change is necessary in all aspects of our lives; we need to do better, be better. You can never go wrong being kind.

So many people want to flip homes. I speak from experience; the results can be rewarding financially and community-wide. But you have to have a thick skin and a kind heart, and a desire to create win/win relationships. I often drive neighborhoods looking for homes that need care and repairs or are obviously vacant. I check the tax records to determine ownership and where the owner resides and use the internet to see what status is on the home. It could be an estate of an out-of-town relative that does not want to live there, but the home is in too poor a condition to sell.

This opens up an opportunity to create a win/win for the out-of-town family and yourself. If you can purchase the property 'as is' and relieve their financial burden, they can receive fair compensation quickly and without having the continuing stress of insurance, tax payments, electricity, heat, lawn maintenance, and snow removal. How do you know how much to offer to pay is determined by the ARV, the After-Repair Value, and offering between 40-70% depending on how much work is needed to make the home marketable. Another way to prospect homes is to have yourself added to wholesalers buying lists to access discounted properties. Find a real estate agent that specializes in investment properties. Do mailings or door-hanger advertisements on zip codes in your desired neighborhoods.

The After-Repair Value is determined by finding comparable homes in size (+/- 150 sq ft.) with the same number of bedrooms and baths, garage space, in the same school district, and in neighborhoods that are already improved.

One important thing to remember is to give the house the repairs and improvements the future buyer will expect. Use caution not to over-improve; this can price your prospective buyer right out of the home. Keep in mind what the other homes in the neighborhood are selling for and the amenities they possess. My niche is first-time buyer homes. These homes usually are in established neighborhoods where revitalization is taking place. Banks are often hesitant to loan money on these properties due to the condition of the home, and will not loan the repair costs, so usually alternative financing may be needed, especially on your first flip home.

You can check into using investments from some types of IRA's using your own savings, taking a home equity loan, and asking family or friends to invest. People have been having success using Crowdfunding. Consider Hard Money lenders or asking people if they would like to make a higher percentage rate on a short-term loan than they could traditionally receive, one that is backed by the collateral of the physical real estate. I suggest attending real estate investor meetings and asking what creative financing people are using and providing now.

For the next step, you need to assemble a team. You need to find a real estate agent if you are not one yourself. You need to create a list of sub-contractors: framers, finishers, flooring specialists, painters, electricians, plumbers, HVAC techs, roofers, landscapers, grass-mowing and snow-plowing people, sheetrock hangers, and tapers. Many of you are looking to do much of these tasks yourself, but do not underestimate the value of prescreened professionals in your contacts on your phone for if or when you need them. Always hire licensed professionals to do any work that will require a permit and inspection. Yes, it is more expensive to hire licensed professionals for these items, but you will be protected from fines, lawsuits, and damage to your reputation, which will all be worth it for peace of mind. Everything else can be learned, YouTubed, hired out, bartered, or you may find a trusted partner.

Do Not Over-improve! <u>This is worth repeating</u>... *Do Not Over-improve!* This is the biggest mistake new remodelers make. Yes, it would look great to knock down the wall from the kitchen to the living area to create an open-concept floor plan. But does this make fiscal sense? Do the other homes in the area have this concept? Is it worth hiring a structural engineer to design the plan for how large and wide the beam needs to be to support the roof if it is a load-bearing wall? You also need to add in the downtime and cost of the permit and sign-off by the inspector and the added cost of ceiling and floor transitions if not already in the budget. Yes, it would look great, but is it what the buyer expects, and is it going to give you the return you need for the added time and expense? Remember, what you want or like is not important. What your buyer wants and can afford is what you need to provide.

I am a firm believer in the CASH-clean, safe, affordable housing method. I am a proponent of reuse, repurpose and recycle of all materials possible. I use Craigslist to purchase many things that still have a lot of life left in them. Never underestimate a good cleaning and a coat of paint.

Always stage the home before photos and putting it on the market. For portability and ease, use furniture that is lightweight and easy to store and carry. My biggest secret is to use raised air mattresses on a platform base. This has saved me thousands of dollars over the years in storage and moving charges. Use on-trend bedding with a more neutral color of comforter with pillows for that pop of color. These beds and spreads can be deflated and stored in provided bags, and all bedding and pillows can be placed in a vacuumed air space bag to keep them clean and together. These can be stored on a shelf in the warehouse with almost no space being consumed vs. storage for traditional mattress sets, beds, and bedding.

Stick with neutral color pallets for paint, but you can always use art, pillows, or accessories to add the current 'wow' color. Clean will sell your home. Sparkling clean windows cannot be underrated.

When you sell your flip home, make sure you look into ways to save money, such as using a 1031 exchange. Possibly ask for a discounted realtor commission from your chosen realtor.

I wish to leave you knowing there is money to be made in real estate. My hope and suggestion to you is that you invest in training for yourself and your team. You will reap the benefits and your team loyalty for years to come. Be a mentor, a trainer, and an active community member. Have a student as a paid intern. When you walk down the sidewalk, be the person who picks up the litter along the way. Plant trees. Reuse, repurpose and recycle. Listen to the ideas of others, create partnerships, offer help where and when you can. *Think outside the box.*

I would like to share a story. I was at a conference in Utah, and a friend and I drove up the mountain to see the Park City lights from above. We got to the top of this long winding road in the dark and parked at the lookout site. My friend commented on how small Park City looked, surrounded by the night's blackness. For whatever reason, all of a sudden, I looked up. I had never seen the sky so clear and so many stars. That moment changed my life. I had been focusing on how small the city looked my whole life, but at that moment, I realized there is no limit, no confines. I realized I was living in the feeling of scarcity, and by just looking up, I was humbled to realize the truth of abundance.

I strive to leave everyone, every place, and everything better than I found them. God Bless.

About Rosie

Rosie Gregerson Schueller helps people find their purpose, and coaches them on how to achieve goals. She spends her time finding distressed real estate and breathing new life into them.

Rosie Schueller is a philanthropist to causes dear to her, working to fund shelters for families escaping domestic violence and even saving Orangutans in Borneo. She has a degree in Education and holds an MBA. Rosie is a Certified Canfield Trainer and Speaker and a licensed real estate broker and building contractor.

Rosie is married to her husband Jim, and they have son Tanner, who is creative and funny and makes the world a better place, and an adopted golden retriever named Cooper. She enjoys spending time with her friends and family, dividing her time between her homes they built in both Minnesota and their Lake home in Wisconsin. Rosie strives to always leave everything and everyone better than she found them. Above all else, she is a Christian and knows she is blessed.

To reach Rosie:
- Rosie@SchuellerVentures.com
- www.SchuellerVentures.net

CPSIA information can be obtained
at www.ICGtesting.com
Printed in the USA
LVHW081359170921
698100LV00016B/532/J